D0458756

# Baby Boomers and Beyond

## Tapping the Ministry Talents and Passions of Adults over Fifty

### Amy Hanson

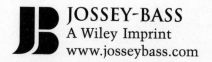

JOSSEY-BASS
A Wiley Imprint
www.josseybass.com

Copyright © 2010 by Amy Hanson. All rights reserved.

Published by Jossey-Bass
A Wiley Imprint
989 Market Street, San Francisco, CA 94103-1741—www.josseybass.com

No part of this publication may be reproduced, stored in a retrieval system, or transmitted in any form or by any means, electronic, mechanical, photocopying, recording, scanning, or otherwise, except as permitted under Section 107 or 108 of the 1976 United States Copyright Act, without either the prior written permission of the publisher, or authorization through payment of the appropriate per-copy fee to the Copyright Clearance Center, Inc., 222 Rosewood Drive, Danvers, MA 01923, 978-750-8400, fax 978-646-8600, or on the Web at www.copyright.com. Requests to the publisher for permission should be addressed to the Permissions Department, John Wiley & Sons, Inc., 111 River Street, Hoboken, NJ 07030, 201-748-6011, fax 201-748-6008, or online at www.wiley.com/go/permissions.

Readers should be aware that Internet Web sites offered as citations and/or sources for further information may have changed or disappeared between the time this was written and when it is read.

Limit of Liability/Disclaimer of Warranty: While the publisher and author have used their best efforts in preparing this book, they make no representations or warranties with respect to the accuracy or completeness of the contents of this book and specifically disclaim any implied warranties of merchantability or fitness for a particular purpose. No warranty may be created or extended by sales representatives or written sales materials. The advice and strategies contained herein may not be suitable for your situation. You should consult with a professional where appropriate. Neither the publisher nor author shall be liable for any loss of profit or any other commercial damages, including but not limited to special, incidental, consequential, or other damages.

Jossey-Bass books and products are available through most bookstores. To contact Jossey-Bass directly call our Customer Care Department within the U.S. at 800-956-7739, outside the U.S. at 317-572-3986, or fax 317-572-4002.

Jossey-Bass also publishes its books in a variety of electronic formats. Some content that appears in print may not be available in electronic books.

**Library of Congress Cataloging-in-Publication Data**

Hanson, Amy, date.
    Baby boomers and beyond : tapping the ministry talents and passions of adults over fifty / Amy Hanson. – 1st ed.
        p. cm. – (Leadership network titles)
    Includes bibliographical references and index.
    ISBN 978-0-470-50079-8 (cloth); 9-780-470-63292-5 (ebk); 9-780-470-63293-2 (ebk); 9-780-470-63294-9 (ebk)
1. Church work with the baby boom generation.  2. Church work with older people.  I. Title.
    BV4435.H36 2010
    259'.3–dc22                                         2010008092

Printed in the United States of America
FIRST EDITION
HB Printing     10 9 8 7 6 5 4 3 2 1

# Leadership Network Titles

*The Blogging Church: Sharing the Story of Your Church Through Blogs,* Brian Bailey and Terry Storch

*Church Turned Inside Out: A Guide for Designers, Refiners, and Re-Aligners,* Linda Bergquist and Allan Karr

*Leading from the Second Chair: Serving Your Church, Fulfilling Your Role, and Realizing Your Dreams,* Mike Bonem and Roger Patterson

*The Way of Jesus: A Journey of Freedom for Pilgrims and Wanderers,* Jonathan S. Campbell with Jennifer Campbell

*Leading the Team-Based Church: How Pastors and Church Staffs Can Grow Together into a Powerful Fellowship of Leaders,* George Cladis

*Organic Church: Growing Faith Where Life Happens,* Neil Cole

*Church 3.0: Upgrades for the Future of the Church,* Neil Cole

*Off-Road Disciplines: Spiritual Adventures of Missional Leaders,* Earl Creps

*Reverse Mentoring: How Young Leaders Can Transform the Church and Why We Should Let Them,* Earl Creps

*Building a Healthy Multi-Ethnic Church: Mandate, Commitments, and Practices of a Diverse Congregation,* Mark DeYmaz

*Leading Congregational Change Workbook,* James H. Furr, Mike Bonem, and Jim Herrington

*The Tangible Kingdom: Creating Incarnational Community,* Hugh Halter and Matt Smay

*Baby Boomers and Beyond: Tapping the Ministry Talents and Passions of Adults over Fifty,* Amy Hanson

*Leading Congregational Change: A Practical Guide for the Transformational Journey,* Jim Herrington, Mike Bonem, and James H. Furr

*The Leader's Journey: Accepting the Call to Personal and Congregational Transformation,* Jim Herrington, Robert Creech, and Trisha Taylor

*Whole Church: Leading from Fragmentation to Engagement,* Mel Lawrenz

*Culture Shift: Transforming Your Church from the Inside Out,* Robert Lewis and Wayne Cordeiro, with Warren Bird

*Church Unique: How Missional Leaders Cast Vision, Capture Culture, and Create Movement*, Will Mancini

*A New Kind of Christian: A Tale of Two Friends on a Spiritual Journey*, Brian D. McLaren

*The Story We Find Ourselves In: Further Adventures of a New Kind of Christian*, Brian D. McLaren

*Missional Renaissance: Changing the Scorecard for the Church*, Reggie McNeal

*Practicing Greatness: 7 Disciplines of Extraordinary Spiritual Leaders*, Reggie McNeal

*The Present Future: Six Tough Questions for the Church*, Reggie McNeal

*A Work of Heart: Understanding How God Shapes Spiritual Leaders*, Reggie McNeal

*The Millennium Matrix: Reclaiming the Past, Reframing the Future of the Church*, M. Rex Miller

*Shaped by God's Heart: The Passion and Practices of Missional Churches*, Milfred Minatrea

*The Missional Leader: Equipping Your Church to Reach a Changing World*, Alan J. Roxburgh and Fred Romanuk

*Missional Map-Making: Skills for Leading in Times of Transition*, Alan J. Roxburgh

*Relational Intelligence: How Leaders Can Expand Their Influence Through a New Way of Being Smart*, Steve Saccone

*Viral Churches: Helping Church Planters Become Movement Makers*, Ed Stetzer and Warren Bird

*The Externally Focused Quest: Becoming the Best Church for the Community*, Eric Swanson and Rick Rusaw

*The Ascent of a Leader: How Ordinary Relationships Develop Extraordinary Character and Influence*, Bill Thrall, Bruce McNicol, and Ken McElrath

*Beyond Megachurch Myths: What We Can Learn from America's Largest Churches*, Scott Thumma and Dave Travis

*The Elephant in the Boardroom: Speaking the Unspoken About Pastoral Transitions*, Carolyn Weese and J. Russell Crabtree

# CONTENTS

# ABOUT LEADERSHIP NETWORK

Leadership Network, an initiative of OneHundredX, exists to honor God and serve others by investing in innovative church leaders who impact the Kingdom immeasurably.

Since 1984, Leadership Network has brought together exceptional leaders, who are focused on similar ministry initiatives, to accelerate their impact. The ensuing collaboration—often across denominational lines—provides a strong base from which individual leaders can better analyze and refine their individual strategies. Creating an environment for collaborative discovery, dialogue, and sharing encourages leaders to extend their own innovations and ideas. Leadership Network further enhances this process through the development and distribution of highly targeted ministry tools and resources—including video, podcasts, concept papers, special research reports, e-publications, and books like this one.

With Leadership Network's assistance, today's Christian leaders are energized, equipped, inspired—and better able to multiply their own dynamic Kingdom-building initiatives.

In 1996 Leadership Network partnered with Jossey-Bass, a Wiley imprint, to develop a series of creative books that would provide thought leadership to innovators in church ministry. Leadership Network Publications present thoroughly researched and innovative concepts from leading thinkers, practitioners, and pioneering churches. The series collectively draws from a wide range of disciplines, with individual titles providing perspective on one or more of five primary areas:

- Enabling effective leadership
- Encouraging life-changing service
- Building authentic community
- Creating Kingdom-centered impact
- Engaging cultural and demographic realities

For additional information on the mission or activities of Leadership Network, please contact:

Leadership Network
2626 Cole Avenue, Suite 900
Dallas, Texas 75204
800-765-5323
www.leadnet.org
client.care@leadnet.org

# ACKNOWLEDGMENTS

My heart is full of gratitude to many people who have influenced me in the writing of this book.

Don Wilcox: You pushed and prodded me, encouraged me, and opened doors to me. God obviously put you in my path in order to spur this ministry on to the next level. There are numerous places in this book where your insights and ideas are visible. I am indebted to you.

My friends at Leadership Network who have helped me in my writing: Warren Bird, Stephanie Plagens, Bonnie Randle, and Mark Sweeney—thank you!

All the church leaders and pastors who have shared their stories and insights with me: Paul Stetler, Chris Holck, Rosayln "Bambi" Encarnacion, John Coulombe, Rod Toews, Richard and Leona Bergstrom, Dave McElheran, Woods Watson, Dwight Munn, Earl Ferguson, Mopsy Andrews, Carolyn Lovelady, Dave McClamma, Max Pyron, Janice Beyers, Dan Allen, Pete Menconi, Wendell Nelson, Kevin Burdette . . . the list could go on and on. Thank you for sharing a similar passion for older adult ministry.

Sheryl Fullerton and Alison Knowles at Jossey-Bass: This was my first publishing experience, and you have made it a great one. Thank you for your constructive criticism, gentle feedback, and cheers of encouragement throughout this process.

My mom and dad, Dennis and Linda Befort, who are leading-edge boomers themselves: Thanks for letting me bounce ideas off you and for letting me go forward in this ministry, even when you thought it was a crazy thing for a twenty-year-old to do.

And thank you for babysitting, cooking, and praying! I also thank my sister, Ann McNellis, for help with editing, and my brother, Allen Befort, for being willing to talk ministry stuff with me.

My in-laws, Marilyn and Bill Mueksch: I so appreciate your willingness to play with Ella and Eli while I wrote. And Bill, thank you for sharing your books on aging with me.

Ella: We may never know how much you have influenced this book through your prayers and encouragement. When I would get discouraged, you would say, "Mommy, just trust God for what to write!" Thanks for being patient while I spent so much time in front of my computer. You are a precious gem!

Eli: You were my constant companion, growing inside of me as I wrote the manuscript for this book. I'm so grateful you are in my life!

Jon: You were always the one to say, "You should do this!" "You can do this!" Thanks for offering your suggestions, helping me through the hard parts, and carrying so much of the load on the home front while I completed this project. "Thank you" is truly not enough.

And finally, Bob Murphy (1930–1998), who was willing to take a twenty-year-old college student under his wing and mentor her in older adult ministry. I know God used you to lead me in this ministry.

# INTRODUCTION: REINVENTING MINISTRY WITH OLDER ADULTS

It was a hot and humid summer evening in rural Iowa. I had been asked to meet with the leaders of a particular church to help them set a direction for a brand-new senior adult ministry. The sixty-five-year-old senior pastor had led this church to grow from 150 to over 550 regular attenders in his thirty-four-year tenure, and he would soon be phasing out of this leadership role and taking on a part-time role as the minister of senior adults.

It was apparent to me from a previous visit to the church, a few conversations on the phone, and a casual dinner that these leaders had some assumptions as to what this ministry would be. Perhaps visiting the elderly. Planning dinners and parties for the senior members of the congregation. Hosting Bible studies in local retirement homes. Obviously some very good and traditional ideas.

But as I began the meeting, I told them the most important question to answer in the room that night was not which activities or programs to plan but rather who it was they really wanted to reach. What did this person look like? They could say it was a ministry for adults over sixty, but the numerical age alone was not descriptive enough. My task was to paint a few verbal pictures of different older adults so that they would be better equipped to define whom the ministry was intended to reach.

We all have ideas that come to mind when we think of the later years of life, and we all have a way that we define "age." As you think about your current ideas with regard to older adult ministry, consider these snapshots of three different categories of older adults.

One group of older adults is the frail elderly. We might say they are in the eighty-five-plus age range, though using chronological age as a defining mark is not always appropriate. This is a group of people whose health is a primary factor in their lives. In some cases, they can no longer drive, and they may be homebound and suffering from isolation. Ministry opportunities with this group abound. Visitation, driving them to appointments, cleaning their homes, and responding to their physical needs are just a few of the ways to serve this segment of the population. Ministry with the sick and frail is also a biblical mandate found in James 1:27 and Isaiah 1:17, where we are instructed to care for orphans and widows.

A second set of older adults can be identified as seniors. In assigning numerical ages, we might identify this group as being seventy (or even seventy-five) to eighty-four years old. There's a good chance these folks are retired, though still engaged in activities, and they may prefer to drive only in daylight. These adults may be experiencing multiple losses—the loss of a spouse, loss of their own health, and even the loss of friends and siblings. This has been the target group for a traditional senior adult ministry. Historically, these ministries have been characterized by trips and fellowship-centered programs. And yet there is a great opportunity to engage people in this age group in meaningful service opportunities as well as encouraging them to reach out to their unchurched peers. A number of churches throughout the country are doing innovative ministry with this segment of the population, and this is certainly a worthy age group in which to invest time and ministry efforts. But this particular group of older adults (often referred to as the "builder generation") does not have the same characteristics or needs as the third set of older adults.

The third group describes who I am referring to in this book as the "new old." I first heard this term used by my friend and colleague in older adult ministry, John Coulombe, to describe an emerging group of older adults who approach aging differently than previous generations.

Taking a purely chronological look, this is the set of adults ranging in age from fifty to seventy. The majority of people in this age group are baby boomers; a small proportion are just slightly older. This is an enormous demographic, especially when you consider that the baby boomers alone consist of seventy-eight million Americans.

These adults are dealing with a number of issues, including concerns regarding retirement, grandparenting, caring for aging parents, and preparing for their own aging. For the most part, they are healthy, active, and quite capable of serving God in some remarkable ways. They have more discretionary time and may naturally be searching for what their purpose will be as they begin to phase out of their careers. They have a strong desire to not "get old" and are doing all they can to stay young.

This book will primarily focus on that third group of older adults. I will use a variety of different terms to describe this particular generation, including baby boomers, leading-edge boomers, older adults, adults over fifty, and the new old. It's hard to put rigid numerical ages on the people we will be discussing because health and attitude play a tremendous role in how people age. There are ninety-year-olds who still drive a car and are active from dawn until dusk, and then there are sixty-year-olds who are confined to home or even a nursing home.

With that said, we will discover that generational differences can have an effect on how aging is perceived and what ministry with older adults looks like. So please hear me loud and clear: the ages we assign to people are merely numbers, and they don't completely define the people themselves. We are talking about a philosophy of ministry in which older adults are engaged in meaningful service and Kingdom impact that have the ability to transcend age.

In Part One of the book, we'll look at the urgency of this ministry and why our churches cannot afford to ignore this generation of people who are marching into the later years of life.

We'll also take a hard look at some of the negative stereotypes that have permeated our society, our people, our churches, and even our own attitudes.

In Part Two, we'll dive deep into three of the main issues on the minds of boomers: staying young, juggling multiple relationships, and redefining retirement. If we want to reach individuals both in the church and outside the church, we've got to understand who they are and their pressing concerns.

Finally, Part Three will be devoted to the implications of an aging population for the church. How do we do ministry? What should be the focus? Where do we put our energy? And most important, how do we harness the potential of this new generation? These are questions for all who want to be serious about ministering with aging boomers.

This is a book for senior pastors, leaders, and primary influencers in the church who desire to be equipped for the biggest demographic reality shaping our culture. As you read, you will discover connections between the dynamics of aging and the real-world experience of ministry in the local church. This book will not provide you with a step-by-step approach for starting a boomer ministry, although I have included numerous examples from churches across the country to suggest practical ways to put these principles in motion.

Primarily, my hope is that this book will serve as a wake-up call to one of the greatest realities facing the church today, both in America and around the world. The principles we will discuss are transferable and applicable for churches of all sizes, in all communities, all over the globe.

I warn you that portions of these chapters aren't easy to read because they force us to shine a light on our own attitudes regarding aging and perhaps even confront attitudes we need to change. But that's OK. That's the kind of work God does, and the work He wants to do in our churches often starts with the leaders. It's both exciting and scary because the potential for ministry is endless and a number of needs are just waiting to be addressed.

Let's go back to that summer night in Iowa. After presenting the three different groups of older adults and asking some reflective questions, I began to see light bulbs turn on in the minds of these leaders. I heard comments like "She's talking about us" and "This is a complete paradigm shift." And then one man had the courage to say, "I think we should focus our ministry efforts on the fifty-to-seventy age group. We have just a short window of time to catch these people as they are planning how they will spend their retirement years and how they will invest the rest of their lives." Others nodded in agreement, and one said, "These are the folks who can be the best servants, the best workers to do the ministry with the two older age groups." And then with excitement another voice said, "And we need those in their fifties and sixties to be mentoring young couples." And the enthusiasm began to grow. And leaders began to dream. And the old aging paradigms began to change. And the door flew wide open to the ministry possibilities waiting to be mined within this generation.

What happened among those leaders is what I hope happens on your journey through the pages of this book: that we will grasp a new vision of what older adult ministry could be. What older adult ministry could be if we let go of the negative stereotypes associated with aging. What it could be if we started recognizing the potential for Kingdom impact lying dormant among older adults. What it could be if we reshaped our churches to be more intergenerational, with a focus on reaching all age groups, equally. What it could be to see people in their fifties, sixties, and seventies finding their way to God and grabbing hold of the salvation only He offers. What it could be to call people out of a self-focused retirement lifestyle and into something much greater.

Let's dream about what could be—and then let's go make it a reality. Seventy-eight million boomers are waiting.

*To Ella, who prayed every day that God would give
Mommy the words to write. I love you.*

# Part One

# READY FOR MORE: THE NEW OLD

# 1

# A WAKE-UP CALL
# FOR THE CHURCH

## A Reality We Can't Ignore

It was the mid-1950s, and millions of baby boomers were nearing adolescence. Never before had there been such an influx of young people who were drastically shaping the culture. And the church was unprepared. Youth ministry expert Mark Senter writes, "The post-war baby boom caught the church without a strategy for dealing with the sudden influx of people whom the media began to call 'teenagers.'"[1]

These young baby boomers represented a huge untapped resource for the church, and some people began to work nationally at convincing church leaders that youth ministry was vitally important. These entrepreneurs created a sense of urgency among churches to reach out to this young generation before it was too late.

This idea caught on, in part because of the bulging number of teenagers who were alive. Today, most churches have a youth minister as a part of their staff, and often it is the second or third position they add after the senior pastor. Youth ministry has become a popular degree of study in most Bible colleges and seminaries across the country. It is an expected element of our current church culture.

These baby boomers who revolutionized youth ministry are now entering their fifth and sixth decades of life. They are marching into their later years at an unprecedented rate. And the urgency of ministry with them is just as great as when they were young—perhaps even greater.

The stakes are high. There is much to be gained for Christ or much to be lost. And it starts with whether or not we choose to ignore or embrace this aging reality.

## Longevity and the Growth of the Older Population

For nearly a century, there has been an upward trend in people living longer and the older population growing. In 1900, 4 percent of the population was over age sixty-five; in 2001, the figure was 12 percent; and the projection for 2030 is that the proportion of people over sixty-five will rise to 20 percent.[2]

Take a look at some other statistics. You may have seen these before or heard them discussed on a news program, but try to look with fresh eyes at these astronomical numbers and really let them soak in.

- Americans sixty-five and older are the fastest-growing segment of the population.
- In the past century, the number of Americans over age sixty-five has increased twelvefold (from 3.1 million to 37.9 million).[3]
- By the year 2030, there will be 72.1 million people in America over the age of sixty-five.[4]
- An American turns sixty every seven seconds.[5]

### Life Expectancy

One of the primary reasons we have so many older adults is that life expectancy is increasing. This is known as the squaring of the pyramid. Take a look at Figures 1.1 and 1.2. In the early 1900s, the number of adults living into their later years was small. Today, people are living much longer.

Life expectancy is the *average* number of years of life remaining at birth or from some particular age in a given population. For instance, in the early 1900s, life expectancy in the United

States was forty-seven. This meant that when a baby was born, he could expect to live until the age of forty-seven. In the year 2009, life expectancy for a Caucasian baby was approximately seventy-eight years (and this number is projected to rise).

That life expectancy in 1900 was forty-seven did not mean that forty-six-year-olds began to fear they were soon going to die. Nor did a forty-year-old look like an old person, with white hair and wrinkles. There simply weren't all that many people who remained alive until old age. The difference today is that we are seeing the majority of people in industrialized nations living into the later years of life.

A reduction in infant deaths, immunizations for children, advances in medicine, and overall better health care have been some of the primary factors contributing to the growth in life expectancy. In addition, people are better educated about their health and are practicing better habits that lead to longer lives. Fewer employees are dying in work-related accidents, and work environments are generally cleaner and safer than in the past. All of these factors contribute to people living longer.

## Birth Rate

A second reason we are experiencing such growth in the older population has to do with the birth rate. I've pointed out that the percentage of older people is on the rise. Percentages are determined by the composition of the entire population. So if a lot of babies are born, this will raise the percentage of young people and lower the percentage of older people. On the other hand, if the birth rate is low, this will result in a larger percentage of older adults.

The post–World War II baby boom initially drove the percentage of old people in America down because so many young people were suddenly part of the mix. The generation following the boomers was much smaller, fewer babies were born, and the result is now a higher percentage of older adults.

## Figure 1.1 Age Profile of the U.S. Population, c. 1900

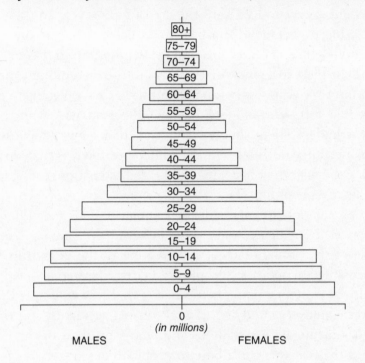

MALES                    FEMALES

## Global Aging

The growth of the aging population is not unique to the United States. It is being felt by many industrialized nations. Japan is recognized as the world's fastest-aging society; by the year 2015, fully 25 percent of its population will be over sixty-five. Other developed countries, including Italy, Germany, and Greece, have a high percentage of older adults. It's interesting to note that even in developing countries, the number of older adults is growing. Such countries as Colombia and India are experiencing a rapid increase in people over the age of sixty-five.

The U.S. Census Bureau projects that across the world, by the year 2018 (if not sooner), people over the age of sixty-five will outnumber children under the age of five. For the first time

**Figure 1.2 Age Profile of the U.S. Population, c. 2000**

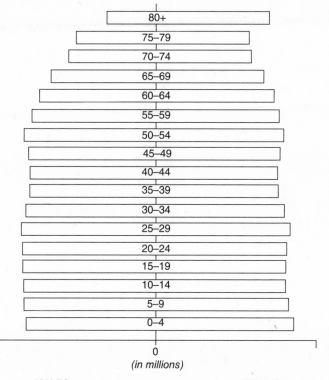

| 80+ |
| 75–79 |
| 70–74 |
| 65–69 |
| 60–64 |
| 55–59 |
| 50–54 |
| 45–49 |
| 40–44 |
| 35–39 |
| 30–34 |
| 25–29 |
| 20–24 |
| 15–19 |
| 10–14 |
| 5–9 |
| 0–4 |

0
*(in millions)*

MALES                    FEMALES

*Source, Figures 1.1 and 1.2:* S. J. Olshansky, "The Demography of Aging," in Christine K. Cassell and others, eds., *Geriatric Medicine: An Evidence-Based Approach*, 4th ed. (New York: Springer-Verlag, 2003), pp. 39–40.

in history, there will be more older adults than children on the planet.

People everywhere are recognizing the growth of the older population and considering how to both accommodate and capitalize on this phenomenon. One example comes from the city of Shanghai, China, which has recently decided to relax the law permitting couples to have only one child in order to increase the pool of individuals available to provide care for the growing numbers of older adults. Seoul, South Korea, is also looking for ways to boost the birth rate in order to help balance the population. Some government offices in Seoul plan to provide up to 30 million won, equivalent to about U.S. $25,500, to families having three or more children.[6]

## How Does Age Affect the Church?

We can talk forever about numbers and statistics and the causes for these trends. What does all of this really mean for those of us living in the twenty-first century who care about Christ and His church?

First, it is no accident that God has allowed such a large number of older people to be alive at this moment in time. In His great sovereignty and wisdom, He chose this time to raise up an army of older adults for His purposes. We must tap into God's plan for the members of this generation, to see them come to Christ, grow in Him, and be engaged in meaningful service.

Second, if we take these statistics seriously, we can see that we are not talking about creating some little subsidiary ministry for a few older people who live in our communities and go to our churches. Rather, we should plan and dream for this to be one of the strategic initiatives of the church. In the past, older adult ministry was not seen as crucial to the mission of the church. As we move into the future, this attitude must change. If we want to be churches and Christians who are in step with the demographic trends of our time, we must respond to this one. It's huge.

Third, this ministry is much bigger than the baby boom generation alone. There are hundreds of thousands of older adults in their late sixties, seventies, and even eighties who are looking at aging in a new way. They are seeking meaning and purpose and are capable of contributing their time and talents to Kingdom efforts.

Fourth, older adulthood is becoming a life stage of its own. With the majority of people born expecting to live into their later years, we have an entirely new season of life. Developmental psychologists used to focus on the changes in childhood and adolescence and then lumped all of adulthood into one category. Now the older years are being perceived as a brand-new stage of life with its own opportunities and challenges—as well as great possibilities for ministry. If we choose to embrace this reality, we have the chance to help define what this new stage of life will be like.

Finally, this is not a ministry for just the United States. Nearly every country in every part of the world is being affected by aging, and opportunities to minister and encourage older adults to live for Christ abound.

## The New Old

To minister effectively with the growing older population, we must understand some common characteristics regarding this new generation of adults.

The baby boom generation includes seventy-eight million people born between 1946 and 1964 and reflects the boom in the birth rate after World War II. This is the largest generation in U.S history and is made up of two cohorts—leading-edge boomers, born between 1946 and 1955, and trailing-edge boomers, born between 1956 and 1964. Leading-edge boomers were influenced by many social movements, including civil rights, modern feminism, antiwar protests, the sexual revolution, and drugs. Today, the majority of leading-edge boomers are facing the empty nest, providing care for aging parents, and dealing with retirement.

Because of their large numbers, as the boomers have progressed through life, their needs and desires have taken center stage. Whether it be the need for more diapers, more schools, or more jobs, this generation has been a driving force behind many of the changes we have experienced in our culture.

As a whole, members of this group were willing to leave behind some of the values of their parents and do things differently. In many ways, they have approached politics, fashion, child rearing, and religion differently than their parents.

It should therefore come as no surprise that they are approaching the later years of life in a different way than the generations before them.

## A Different Perspective

Research sponsored by Merrill Lynch indicated that 70 to 80 percent of boomers want to keep *working* in some fashion after they retire. Interestingly, most of them would like to find different jobs in areas of personal interest where they can make a difference in society. They want work that will allow them the flexibility to travel, spend time with family, participate in leisure activities, and continue learning.

Boomers are also very interested in *staying young*. They plan to remain active and involved with life and don't want to participate in things that suggest they are aging. The idea of sitting in a rocking chair is not appealing to them. One way to see this more clearly is by looking at two general ways in which people age.

Disengagement theory was an early academic theory proposed to explain aging. It stated that the experience of aging involved a mutual withdrawal of the elderly person from society and society from the elder. In my mind, I see images of an old woman being put on a raft and pushed out to sea, never to return again. Disengagement theory isn't quite that drastic, but it does tend to view older people as detaching from this world as they prepare for death.

A second theory that emerged around the same time period as disengagement theory was activity theory. Activity theory stands in complete contrast to disengagement. Proponents of this theory believe that the best approach to aging is staying active. Even if someone's general routine changes—say, from working full time to working part time—the emphasis is still on being involved. Most people today—especially baby boomers—are pro-ponents of this particular theory of aging. Boomers want their later years of life to be very similar to their midlife.

Finally, as boomers approach their later years, they are *searching for purpose*. They may look for purpose through relationships, education, and even leisure pursuits. Others will seek to discover ways they can use their time and experience to serve the needs of those around them. They want their lives, as they get older, to be productive and meaningful—to really count for something. Rather than approaching these years as a time for slowing down, they view this period of life as a time of exciting possibilities.

Although baby boomers do have their own approach to aging, many of their ideas and lifestyle choices with regard to their later years are similar to those of the previous generation. Someone commented to me that even though he was a few years older than the leading-edge boomers, he agreed with many of the thoughts and impressions that boomers have regarding aging. He wants to stay healthy, plans to keep working, and wants to be involved serving and making a significant difference with these years of his life. So the way that boomers view aging will also resonate with people slightly older than those in the boomer age group.

## A New Focus for the Church

Nearly every industry, from travel and leisure to health care, has invested countless hours researching the current demographic trends and the impact they will have on society. Businesses are studying how to develop products that will attract aging people. For example, Chico's is a woman's clothing store that appeals to boomers and older women because it offers stylish clothing that fits more loosely but doesn't look dated. Companies like Johnson & Johnson have begun to design bottles that are easier for arthritic hands to open. The auto industry is studying how to design cars better suited to the growing number of older drivers.

Some states are even redesigning roadway intersections to make them safer for older motorists.

So what about the church? Despite the greater attention being paid by industries to the growth of the older population and the new ways in which boomers are approaching aging, it appears that many churches are ignoring this reality. Why?

**An Obsession with Youth** I was only nine years old, but I still remember the sights and sounds of my dad's fortieth birthday party. Friends and family started showing up at our house wearing all black. Mom pulled a wheelchair out of the closet for Dad to sit in and draped an afghan over his shoulders. Everyone had joined together to mourn the death of my dear father's youth.

For quite some time, our society has not exactly celebrated getting older. Birthday cards lament being "over the hill" or "out to pasture." Adults (especially women) are often unwilling to even tell their age.

It hasn't always been this way. During colonial days, some researchers report, old age was preferred over youth. In meetings, the elderly sat in the positions of highest status. People even wanted to dress in such a way that they looked older. Men's clothing was cut to narrow the shoulders, broaden the waist and hips, and make the spine look bent. Women wore long dresses, and both genders wore white wigs.[7]

As the United States (and other countries) became more industrialized, the value attached to the elderly began to wane. Scientific knowledge grew, technology improved, and the need for older people to share their wisdom and experience became less important. Over time, being young has become the preferred status.

Today, we live in a culture that values youth, and we are constantly bombarded with the message that being young is what we should strive for. People use makeup, hair color, and other things to maintain a youthful appearance. I have even seen a surge in news articles focused on medical treatments to help people stay young. One recent article spoke of hormone therapy in which women spend as much as $500 per day to inject hormones into their body that will enable them to look and feel younger.[8]

And while most of us would say that this example is pretty drastic, there are ways in which our churches have bought into the same mind-set as society—that younger is somehow better. We proudly communicate that "ours is a church reaching out to young families." And we believe that growing churches are those that are appealing to the younger generation. If there are too many old people in a church, the common thought is that the church must be dying.

Is it possible to be a vibrant, growing, active church that intentionally seeks to reach middle-aged and older adults? Absolutely. But far too many churches in too many communities are failing to take an honest look at their demographics and pay attention to whom God has put in their path. As already noted, the older adult population is growing, meaning that there will be a constant flow of people turning sixty, seventy, and eighty for many years to come. As long as we discover effective ways of reaching these adults, our churches will never have to die.

In 2002, Caloundra Church of Christ in Queensland, Australia, was concerned it would have to close its doors. The church had about sixty people at the time, and the leaders said, "We need a youth minister or we are going to die." Richard Pearce began working with the church first as the interim minister and then later as the full-time minister. As Richard began his ministry, he realized that the church was located in a growing seaside community and therefore would never be forced to close as long as the congregation reached out to the people who were moving into the area.

The coastal community attracts large numbers of retirees each year, as well as young people who are looking for jobs. Within six years, the church had grown to an average of 250 people on a Sunday morning by attracting both the young and the old. Richard explains that the church tries to have a variety of ministries that reach out to both age groups. A volunteer ministry team serves the young adults, and another team focuses on the older adults. There are play groups and socials for young moms in the area and a youth ministry and junior church program. There is an annual senior adult convention, as well as walking groups and other activities for older adults. In many activities, the church makes an effort not to segregate by age but to mix the generations.

Richard estimates that 70 percent of the people attending are over the age of fifty. The congregation has seen young people come to Christ as well as older adults. Richard says, "Many of the adults in their fifties and sixties may have gone to church in the past, but they never realized they could have a personal relationship with God."

**Ageism** Not only is our society obsessed with youth, but we've also grown accustomed and, dare I say, even comfortable with the negative attitudes surrounding aging.

In 2009, the TV competition *Britain's Got Talent* featured a forty-seven-year-old contestant named Susan Boyle. Susan got a lot of media attention because she didn't fit the stereotype of an up-and-coming singing star. She looked middle-aged and dowdy without much fashion sense. When she came onto the stage before the three judges and the large audience, you could sense the skepticism and distaste. The camera even panned to one young woman who was rolling her eyes. You got the impression that people were saying, "Why would someone her age be doing this? What makes her think she stands a chance of being taken seriously?"

The term used to describe the negative attitudes hurled at Susan Boyle and many other people in our world is *ageism*. The term was coined in 1969 by Robert Butler, a leader in the field of gerontology, to describe negative perceptions and attitudes toward older people, aging, and old age in general. It's one of the reasons why the church may be ignoring the aging population.

At its worst, ageism, like racism or sexism, is a form of discrimination. It's devaluing someone because of age.

Maybe you are saying, "Hey, wait just a minute! We value everyone in our church." I believe we want to value everyone, but often one age group is emphasized more than another.

I know of a large and growing American church that puts a strong emphasis on missions. Just before the 2008 Summer Olympics were to be held in Beijing, this church's older adult ministry began to invite older adults to be a part of a team that would travel overseas and do ministry during the Olympics. Twenty-four willing and able fifty-plus age adults signed up for this endeavor. They were excited about working in an orphanage in China and providing other services to people in need of the love of Christ.

The missions team at the church, including the missions pastor, agreed to let the group go but was unwilling to list the team in the missions brochure or to include them in the formal introduction and prayer service for short-term missionaries. In short, the missions team said, "Sure, they can go, but we aren't going to back them with financial help, public prayer support, or recognition."

More conversations revealed that the committee was concerned that one of the older members might fall ill or that the older people wanted to go on the trip merely for sightseeing. So in other words, these committee members held some ageist attitudes—that older people are sickly and only interested in leisure activities and that mission trips of this sort should be left to the young.

Before you go shaking your head in judgment at this church, would you be willing to take a hard look at yourself? Have you ever given time in the Sunday service to a high school youth group who went to Mexico? Has the congregation listened to the participants' testimonies and applauded their efforts? Have you given the same amount of platform time to a group of older adults who have gone on a mission trip or participated in a significant service project? Does your staff or even your budget reflect which age group you value most? Do you ever neglect to ask the input of older church members because you believe they will not have much to offer? Ageism has affected all of us. It's crept into our churches without our recognizing it.

Unfortunately, older adults themselves have bought into the negative images of aging. In fact, Linda Woolf of Webster University in Saint Louis, Missouri, said that the greatest limitation facing older adults is not mental or physical handicaps but the negative stereotypes that exist regarding aging. This is a main obstacle to older adults' continuing to grow in the Lord and serve Him to their fullest capacity. Many of them believe the lies that they no longer have something to offer or contribute.

Although ageism is most often associated with older adults, it is technically descriptive of any judging on the basis of age. Young people can experience ageism just as older adults can. In 1 Timothy 4:12, when Paul instructs Timothy not to let anyone look down on him because he is young, Paul is telling Timothy not to let ageism affect the work God wants him to do. This is the same message the church needs to proclaim today regarding the later years of life. If Paul were to visit our churches, he might say, "Don't let anyone look down on you because you are older. Do what God has called you to do!"

Just as we should strive to become churches that do not put limits on people because of their race or gender, we must work just as hard not to restrict the potential of adults because of their age.

## The Time Is Now

At the beginning of this chapter, I quoted Mark Senter, who said that when boomers were advancing in record numbers into their teenage years, the church was caught off guard, without a strategy to reach this group. My fear is that unless the church wakes up to the aging population, we will once again fail to be ready for what is about to hit in full force. We simply cannot afford to ignore this issue.

For one thing, this new generation of older adults represents a huge network of potential Kingdom laborers. Boomers have discretionary time, wisdom, and experience that are too valuable to ignore.

I was reminded of the great impact this generation can make when I talked to David, who works for Voice of the Martyrs, a ministry committed to serving the persecuted church. David was an insurance company vice president when he was laid off at the age of fifty-six. He wasn't planning to retire at the time and attempted to find work with some other company, but God had different plans for him. Even before losing his job, David had been exposed through a newsletter to Voice of the Martyrs and its work to help Christians around the world who were living out their faith and often persecuted for their beliefs. He began volunteering for the organization as a speaker and even traveled overseas to further the group's efforts. The ministry soon became a burning passion within his soul. Nearly four years after leaving his corporate job, while he was in China serving with Voice of the Martyrs, he received word that one of the ministry's key leaders had died in a car accident. The group immediately asked David to replace him.

When other sixty-year-olds might be settling into retirement or looking forward to more time with grandchildren, David and his wife uprooted themselves from the home and community where they had spent much of their lives. They left behind their adult children and grandchildren, aging parents, friends, and church. They moved several states away to a small community where Voice of the Martyrs has its headquarters. And there they started a new life and ministry.

David's business experience and organizational skills make him well suited for the managerial role in which he is now serving. He confessed that he makes about 25 percent of the income he made in his corporate job. But he was quick to tell me he would be happy to do the job for free. He is passionate about the ministry and the work God is doing and is using his energy for the cause of Christ.

We could travel the country and find other stories like David's. People who in their middle and later years are choosing to do something significant that is advancing God's mission in this world. However, I know there could be many, many more adults unleashed into meaningful ministry if the church would begin to call people in their fifties, sixties, and seventies out of a leisure-focused life and into one of service. Imagine the impact to be made on our world. Imagine the yet-to-be-discovered ministries that would reach out to people who are hurting. We need to be leaders that raise the expectation of how older adults are to spend their later years.

A second implication to consider in ministry with this generation is the number of older adults who are lost, without hope, in need of a relationship with Jesus Christ. If we continue to focus all of our efforts on reaching a younger generation for Christ and ignore the older generation, millions of people will face an uncertain eternity.

To begin to love boomers, we must jump into their world. We have to understand their daily needs, interests, and burdens. As boomers search for meaning and purpose in their lives, we offer the only lasting purpose that exists. Recognizing their needs, issues, and desires will be the first steps in loving them and hopefully being used by God to point them to Christ.

Finally, the church has a moment in time, right now, to create a new paradigm for aging. A biblical, God-honoring view of aging. Yes, culture does focus on the young and ageist attitudes abound—but we can be a force that stands counter culture. We can show the world what it means to value people of all ages, rather than marginalizing certain segments of the population. We can communicate that God has a purpose and a specific role for everyone to play, regardless of age.

I think it's going to be an exciting, challenging, and rewarding ride. Won't you join me?

# 2

# NOT WHAT YOU THOUGHT

## New Ways to Think About Aging

It happens nearly every time. I'm at a social function or a church dinner or even a family reunion and the question "What do you do?" is asked, to which I respond, "I work in the area of older adult ministry." And then—it's occurred so often I've come to expect it—people start discussing with me stories and issues related to nursing homes.

It's never easy for me to turn the conversation toward a broader picture of aging because I don't want to minimize the valuable ministry and work that our most frail elders need. The issue of caring for the forgotten in long-term care institutions is very important, and I personally spend a portion of my time serving in this arena.

However, the fact that so many people associate the word *old* with frailty demonstrates that many in our society have a rather shortsighted view of the experience of aging. The reality is that most older adults are quite active. On any given day, fewer than 5 percent of people over sixty-five are in a long-term care facility,[1] and more than 80 percent of people over sixty-five are capable of carrying out the normal activities of daily life—things like cooking a meal, going shopping, getting dressed, and managing money.[2] And even beyond these basic things, many older adults participate in a wide variety of work and leisure pursuits.

## Myths of Aging

One of the greatest challenges that the church faces in regard to the coming age wave is learning to let go of a vast number of negative stereotypes associated with aging and replace them with proven research and biblical truth.

The only way to begin this process is by debunking the myths that have pervaded our society and our churches. We'll never successfully create life-changing older adult ministries if we don't first take a hard look at some of the stereotypes we ourselves may buy into.

## Myth 1: Most Older Adults Are Unable to Adapt to Change

I'm sure you've heard it before; perhaps you've even said it yourself. "She's so stuck in her ways, you'll never get her to go along with that." As church leaders, much of our job revolves around helping people navigate through change. It may be personal change, such as the transition from being a single adult to a married person or from being employed to unemployed. We also lead people through corporate change, such as changing from pews to chairs or from traditional music to contemporary.

Typically, any change is met with some resistance because change signifies loss. It's something new and different. Even good change, such as the birth of a baby or the hiring of an additional staff member, causes people to have to adapt.

Interestingly, research has shown there is not a strong correlation between age and our ability to change.[3] Being able to change has more to do with our own temperament and whether or not change has been easy for us throughout our lives. I have a friend whose ten-year-old son has always struggled with change. His parents must take the time to prepare him if something is not going to happen as it usually does, such as eating dinner at a later hour or needing to sleep in a different room. In contrast, some kids couldn't care less about changes and actually find it an exciting adventure when things are done differently. This ability to adapt to change, either with ease or with difficulty, travels with us throughout our lives. Those who struggled with change when they were younger are more likely to have a hard time with change as they grow older.

For the most part, older adults have endured a tremendous amount of change throughout their lives: raising children, persevering through financial difficulty, dealing with the death of loved ones—not to mention the technological and cultural changes they have successfully embraced. Most important, God is in the business of changing people's lives. Through His Holy Spirit, He transforms, molds, shapes, alters, and renews the hearts and minds of people, regardless of age.

Helping individuals navigate through change begins with listening to their feelings and attempting to understand their lives. Aging is characteristically a season of loss: loss of friends that move away or die, loss of physical health, loss of a job to go to every day, and so on. When we experience multiple losses, we naturally try to hold on to something that is a constant, something that remains the same. For many people, their familiar church experiences may be what they hold on to.

Gordon MacDonald, in his fictional book *Who Stole My Church?* tells the story of a group of church members ranging in age from fifty to seventy and how the pastor leads these adults through various changes in the church. During one part of the story, the older adults begin to realize how they have adapted to change in other aspects of their lives yet resisted it in the church. Why? MacDonald writes, "Perhaps . . . we resist change in the church because it seems like the only safe place left in this world where a 'yesterday' still exists when things seemed simpler and more manageable."[4]

Too often leaders think they should do something to pacify the older members of a church. We begin to implement a difficult change and try to find the easiest way to make everyone happy. We'll have a hymn-sing for them or take them on a special trip or hire a part-time staff member to focus on their needs. Unfortunately, all of these efforts communicate that we don't value their opinions or think they are capable of handling a change.

One church I am familiar with hired a new and dynamic pastor who began making some changes: a different style of worship music, a shift from Sunday school classes to small groups, and a new style of preaching. The changes happened quickly, and some of the older adults felt "put on the shelf." Despite a church calendar full of senior adult activities and classes, these older church members were grieving and felt left out.

One of the staff pastors began having conversations over coffee or during meetings, simply to let the older adults share their feelings and concerns. His genuine interest in them and his willingness to be their voice to the church leadership resulted in less criticism and more involvement on the part of these adults.

Dave McClamma, a pastor at First Baptist Church at the Mall, in Lakeland, Florida, suggests two critical ways of helping older adults navigate through church change. First, communicate with them constantly. Talking and listening are keys to showing respect. Second, involve the older adults in the ministry. Rather than searching for some social activity to make them happy, help them find a key place where they can contribute to the mission. It's much easier for people to criticize and feel left out if they are sitting on the sidelines. Individuals who are actively involved in making a difference are more apt to accept the changes.

Listening, showing respect, and getting people involved will go a long way toward helping a person embrace change. People *can* change. It may not always be easy, but it is possible.

## Myth 2: Older Workers Cannot Work as Effectively as Younger Workers

In the workforce, older employees are thought to be prone to illnesses or accidents, to work less efficiently, to be hard to train, and to lack motivation and imagination. Sometimes we even hear statements in the church like "You should slow down and let the younger ones do it." There is a belief that young people have the energy and the fresh ideas to do a job better, but studies have revealed that older workers tend to be as good as—if not better than—their younger counterparts.[5]

Older adults bring a wealth of experience to most jobs and are likely to be loyal and stable. It is true that physical endurance does decline with age, so some manual jobs may become more difficult; however, the decline is gradual and varies from person to person. On the other hand, jobs that require reflection and creativity may best be done by an older person. New research is demonstrating that our brains actually become more creative with increased age.[6]

Socrates wrote one of his greatest philosophies at age seventy. During his eighties, Frank Lloyd Wright designed arguably his most recognized masterpiece, the Guggenheim Museum in New York City. And Noah Webster completed his dictionary at the age of seventy and continued working on revisions to it until just days before his death at age eighty-four.

During biblical times, the expectation was that older adults would remain productive for the Kingdom. Psalm 92:12–14 clearly states, "The righteous will flourish like a palm tree, they will grow like a cedar of Lebanon; planted in the house of the Lord, they will flourish in the courts of our God. They will *still bear fruit* in old age, they will stay fresh and green" (emphasis added). The church has the opportunity to lead the way in demonstrating that older adults can still make meaningful contributions.

I served in ministry with an energetic seventy-year-old man named Joe. He was recently divorced and quickly gravitated to leading a small group with other older single adults. I thought all was well until he confided in me that his heart's passion was with kids. One evening a number of years after I had moved out of state, I was back at this church and happened to walk down the hallway and catch a glimpse of Joe. There he was, high-fiving young boys, hugging them, and expending tons of energy! When I got to him, he flashed me the biggest smile and said, "I love this! This is what I was meant to do!"

Someone could have easily dismissed Joe, thinking he was too old and probably not very effective. A man in his seventies? How would he get on the floor with these kids? Where would he find the energy? Would he be aware of their current issues and needs? Thank goodness there was a leader who recognized the abilities in Joe and helped him find the perfect place to serve.

## Myth 3: Most Older Adults Experience Significant Memory Loss

Spend a few moments glancing at some "over the hill" birthday cards, and chances are you will find some that poke fun at us losing our memory. It seems that when people over forty can't remember a name or recall a conversation, they smile and say, "It must be my age." Unfortunately, behind the jokes are very real fears that advancing age means mental decline. The truth is that fewer than 10 percent of adults over sixty-five suffer from major memory loss.[7] Serious memory problems are the result of something happening in the body, such as Alzheimer's disease, a stroke, or the negative effects of medication. Memory impairment is not a characteristic of normal aging. However, there are some changes that occur in the brain, and thinking processes do slow down.

When studying memory, there are typically two broad categories for us to consider. Long-term memory is the permanent storage site for past experiences. It lets us recall past events, places we have been, and individuals who have been part of our life. Research has proved that long-term memory does not seem to be affected by age. Short-term memory has a limited capacity and keeps things in storage for only a few seconds. This type of memory seems to slow down with age. An older person can retrieve just as many items from short-term memory as a young person, but it may take the older person longer to do so.[8] This is not a reflection of intelligence or ability but simply a manifestation of the mechanics of aging. What an older person brings to the table in terms of experience and wisdom far outweighs any delay in responding.

## Myth 4: Older Adults Are Unable to Learn New Information

My five-year-old daughter is a sponge. She can learn a new Bible verse in a matter of minutes and adds new words to her vocabulary after hearing them read aloud once. When we are young, learning is always occurring, and it takes place quickly. If we could look inside the brain of a young child, we would see new electrical connections forming constantly. As we age, this slows down, and making new connections takes longer. But the wonderful truth about the human brain is that we can learn and grow until the very end of our lives.

Ann was a woman in her seventies who began participating in a nine-month intensive overview of the Bible that our church was offering. She had never grown up reading the Bible for herself or studying it in depth, but she wanted to learn. A few months into the class, I asked how it was going, to which she replied with much enthusiasm, "It's wonderful! I never knew how much was in this book!"

Leaders in the aging field have discovered a few critical factors in creating environments in which older adults can best learn new things. First, adults need to be able to learn at their own pace. In the later years of life, reaction time declines, and we often need more time to complete a task or master a new concept. Second, physical changes in vision and hearing should be considered when creating a learning environment. Glare off a tabletop or an instructor who does not use a microphone can put an older adult at a disadvantage. I read about a gentleman who was having trouble remembering what his wife told him at breakfast and was forgetting important comments made by colleagues at work. His family was very concerned he might have Alzheimer's disease. It turns out he was suffering from some hearing loss, and the problem was easily rectified with hearing aids. Finally, older adults (like all adults) tend to learn best when they are *motivated* to learn. More than once, someone has said to me, "I'm too old to learn the computer." The truth is, the person lacks the desire to learn it; it has nothing to do with age.

## Myth 5: Older Adults Tend to Become More Religious as They Age

Age alone does not automatically make someone interested in matters of faith. A person does not turn sixty-five and then suddenly become tuned in to all things spiritual. A few things contribute to the confusion over this myth. For one, the current older generation attends church more often and professes to be more religious than the younger generation. According to research conducted by the Barna Group, on a typical weekend, 33 percent of mosaics (individuals born between 1984 and 2002), 43 percent of busters (born between 1965 and 1983), 49 percent of boomers (born between 1946 and 1964), and 54 percent of elders (born 1945 and earlier) attend church.[9] Interestingly, the reason for these differences does not correlate with age but rather with the experiences of each particular generation. People who are currently in the older generation have always had a greater propensity toward religious things. It has been a part of their upbringing, and they are carrying this value with them into their later years.

A second point to note is that while many older adults may practice religious habits, such as going to church, not all of them have let the truths of the Bible transform their life.

Gary McIntosh, in his book *One Church, Four Generations*, writes about older adults in their formative years: "A great deal of time was given to Bible study and prayer, and older adults did learn much about the Bible. But there was not always a lot of time given to defining their personal belief system. Many learned the words of the Bible without letting them penetrate their lives."[10]

The reality is that boomer and older adults represent a wide-open door for ministry and evangelism. Not all older people are Christians. Statistics such as "64% of Americans who accept Jesus as their Savior do so before their 18th birthday"[11] have been used to justify why so much energy must be spent on children and youth ministries. And while these are very important areas of work, perhaps the reason for such a low number of conversions in the second half of life is simply because we have not invested time and resources in that particular area.

Bob was nearly eighty years old when he got involved in a small group through a local church. Over time, his eyes opened to the message of the gospel, and he was baptized. He told his friends and family, "All my life, I've known something was missing, and now I know what it was."

Coming to Christ in the later years of life is possible, and it begins with letting go of the myth that the majority of older adults are already believers. "Open your eyes and look at the fields! They are ripe for harvest" (John 4:35).

## Myth 6: Older Adults Want to Relax and Live a Life of Leisure

I teach gerontology (the academic study of aging) to college students. The first day of class, I ask these eighteen- to twenty-year-old students to close their eyes and visualize how they see themselves at the age of eighty. What do they look like? Where are they going to live? Who is going to be in their social world? What kinds of activities will they be doing? They laugh and say, "I'm going to sit in a rocking chair on my porch" or "I plan on playing golf every day." In one particular class session, I asked, "Do any of you see yourselves volunteering when you are older?" and a girl in the back could not believe I was serious. "Why would you do that when you are eighty?!" she exclaimed.

Contrary to the opinion of these students, the vast majority of older adults report that they want to be involved in meaningful and productive activity. Members of the builder generation, born before 1946, have historically been a very civic-minded group and continue to give their time to churches, hospitals, schools, and other community endeavors. Currently, community leaders are wondering, will the baby boom generation, which was stereotypically labeled the "me generation," be as likely to volunteer during the retirement years?

The jury is still out, but the preliminary evidence is good. Greg Baldwin, president of VolunteerMatch, was quoted in the *Wall Street Journal* as saying, "Boomers are far more interested in volunteering than they're given credit for." In fact, VolunteerMatch commissioned an extensive research study in 2006 and discovered that more than half of adults fifty-five and older are interested in volunteering. The challenge is that many of them are having difficulty finding the right opportunity in which to share their skills and experience.[12]

The church has an incredible opportunity to engage this group of people, if we will broaden our perspective on volunteer jobs and a volunteer's capacity. Aging boomers will be looking for ways to use their personal and professional skills. Many of them will want to do more than fold bulletins or staple newsletters. Involving older adults in meaningful service is the foundation on which to build a ministry with the new old. Of all the myths regarding aging, it is imperative that we let go of this one. Retirement is not purely about leisure, and if we fail to recognize this, we will lose an army of people whom God can use to make a tremendous difference.

## Moving Past the Myths

I'll never forget an incident that occurred in my early days of full-time ministry. I was serving as the minister with adults fifty and over at a megachurch in the West, when one of the senior adult men came by the church office and let me have it for not visiting his wife, who had been in the hospital having outpatient surgery. Honestly, being at a big church, I didn't even know she was there, but I took the beating he gave me, and when he left, I laid my head on my desk and cried, feeling like such a failure. Not too much later, one of the administrative assistants heard about what had happened and poked her head into my office to say, "Don't worry about it, Amy; everyone knows that when people get older, they become grumpy and mean."

I hope you will pause and think about that for a moment. Do you believe old age brings out bitterness and anger? What do you think about the later years of life? Are there any of the six myths I've discussed that you have been guilty of believing?

Stereotypes are generalized beliefs that we use to describe certain groups of people. Though I went into detail on six of them, there are many others: old people are bad drivers; old people are bored; old people are not interested in sex; old people are grumpy; and old people are lonely. I'll bet you can even add some of your own to the list.

Stereotypes are formed through the media, our parents, lack of knowledge, and our own experiences. For example, you may have grown up with a neighbor who was a mean old man who sat on his porch and refused to do anything more than yell at the kids who passed by. This experience very well shaped your view of older people. On the other hand, you may have had the sweetest little grandma who baked cookies. Again, as pleasant as this may sound, it still becomes a stereotype if we assume that all old ladies are good cooks who are sweet and kind.

It is natural for us to draw on our own experiences to define people whom we don't really know. But we must be careful our view of others does not hinder our ministry with them. We can break stereotypes and establish new ways of looking at the later years of life if we will be focused and intentional.

## Creating a New Culture

I keep a file in my desk labeled "Senior Heroes," and I try to fill it with news articles and stories about people who have done something significant in the later years of life. The folder includes such stories as a woman who returned to college and graduated with her bachelor's degree at the age of ninety and another who is sixty-five and competes as a slalom skier. All of these help remind me that getting older is not something to fear but to embrace as a God-ordained season of life, a season with great opportunity for continued growth.

Once you begin opening your eyes to the variety of aging experiences occurring in your world, you will begin to notice the stories of older adults living in your community and attending your church. As you hear these stories and begin to share them, you (and the people you serve) will no longer need to cling to stereotypes.

The Plus ministry at Peninsula Covenant Church in Redwood City, California, which caters to people over fifty, publishes a full-color, eight-page newsletter every month that features a church member or couple in the fifty-plus age range on the front cover. An article accompanying the picture gives a short biography of the people and emphasizes their spiritual life and their service to the Lord. The leadership intentionally chooses different ages of older adults, highlighting people in their fifties, sixties, and seventies.[13] Some churches use video technology to record the ways older adults in their communities of faith are growing in their relationship with God and serving Him. These strategic methods shine the spotlight on positive images of aging as opposed to focusing on the myths.

Another way to find models for aging and to refute the lies we've bought into is by highlighting examples from God's Word.

One of my favorites is the story of Caleb found in Joshua 14. Caleb was one of the twelve spies sent by Moses to scout out the land for the Israelites. Ten of the men returned, saying that the land could not be conquered, but Joshua and Caleb had conviction and declared that with God, it was possible. Caleb's faith and determination resulted in a promise from Moses that he would one day settle the hill country of Hebron in the Promised

Land. Unfortunately, Caleb would have to wait forty years as the members of the Israelite nation wandered in the desert due to their unbelief.

Now fast-forward. The forty years have passed, and Caleb is about to claim his promise. Listen to the words of this old man: "Now then, just as the Lord promised, He has kept me alive for forty-five years since the time He said this to Moses, while Israel moved about in the desert. So here I am today, eighty-five years old! I am still as strong today as the day Moses sent me out; I'm just as vigorous to go out to battle now as I was then. Now give me this hill country that the Lord promised me that day" (Joshua 14:10–12).

Here is a man who lived his life to the fullest and did not choose to cave in to any of the myths I've identified. I'm guessing he had some of the usual issues related to aging—perhaps some arthritis and hearing loss—but that did not keep him from working hard and claiming the promise God had for him.

Drawing attention to those making significant contributions in their later years can inspire boomers to see this new season as one of opportunity rather than something to dread.

Another way to move beyond the stereotypes is educating ourselves and others to the realities regarding aging. We have to separate truth from fiction. Jack Rowe and Robert Kahn confirm this in their book, *Successful Aging:*

> Most of us resist replacing myth-based beliefs with science-based conclusions. It involves letting go of something previously ingrained in order to make way for the newly demonstrated facts. Learning something new requires "unlearning" something old and perhaps deeply rooted. Acknowledging the truth about aging in America is critical, however, if we are to move ahead toward successful aging as individuals and as a society. In order to make use of the new scientific knowledge and experience its benefits in our daily lives, we must first "unlearn" the myths of aging.[14]

This "unlearning" can happen in the traditional sense by reading books and articles, taking classes, and attending conferences but it also happens by listening and befriending older adults. Ask them about their experiences regarding aging. What are their feelings? What are their lives really like? It takes effort to consider that the beliefs we have lived by (perhaps some of them mentioned in the myths discussed in this chapter) may in fact not be true.

I recently visited a woman whose frailty deceived me. She was in a wheelchair and looked old, with white hair and deep-set wrinkles, but as I began talking with her, I learned that prior to her having heart surgery a few weeks earlier, she had devoted considerable time every week to the homeless mission in our city—for the past twenty years. She was quite educated as to the needs of homeless people, how we can help them, and the importance of making a difference in their lives. Her room was full of pictures that the children from the mission had colored for her, and it was apparent that she regularly prayed for the ministry.

My few moments with her helped debunk the myth in my mind that older adults want to slow down and focus on themselves. To the contrary, this is a woman still interested in learning, growing, and serving God. Had I not taken the time to talk with her and learn from her, I might still believe some of the myths about aging. This is why, as a gerontology instructor, I require my students to interview older adults and write papers reflecting on what they've observed and how their impressions relate to what they've learned in their textbook. Education happens for us in the same way: studying what the Bible says about aging, reading what the research says, and then testing it through interaction with older people.

Once we begin to reprogram our minds regarding the realities of the later years of life, it will become easier for us to teach these principles to others. Children, young adults, and older adults have all been exposed to the world's lies and need to hear a God-centered viewpoint. Teaching lessons about the myths of aging or writing about these myths in a newsletter or publication is one way to begin changing mind-sets. Encouraging those we lead to study biblical characters such as Simeon and Anna or Abraham and Sarah will help them discover new ways of looking at the later years of life.

First Evangelical Free Church in Fullerton, California, has developed an aging curriculum to use in the children's ministry, where young people can learn about the realities of aging. Part of this curriculum includes older adults attending the children's classes and telling their stories so as to give the young people an inside look into the real lives of older adults, as opposed to what they see in the media.

The formation of intergenerational relationships is an important way to break stereotypes. Whereas a lack of knowledge about aging can reinforce stereotypes, education by itself does not guarantee that a person's negative perceptions of aging will change. It is through relationships that positive attitudes are created. A study conducted in the 1990s revealed that ministers who had a close personal friendship with older members in their congregation had a more positive view of aging than those who did not have a meaningful friendship with an older adult.[15]

In the past, people lived in rural communities where families and neighbors saw each other regularly. Young and old interacted often. In today's culture, we have to be much more intentional about making those relationships happen. Sometimes fear or unmet expectations can cause people of different generations to separate from each other, but finding ways to meaningfully reconnect and learn from one another tends to result in blessing.

## A Change in View

I travel from time to time on airplanes and will leave a city when it is dark and overcast. As the plane climbs, there comes a point when it breaks through the clouds and the sky is blue and the sun is shining. As I look out the window, I can see the gray clouds below us and the clear sky above and around us. So often this is what I need in my own life: simply a different perspective.

For many years, aging has been viewed as something negative. In fact, when the study of gerontology first came on the scene, the emphasis was on the problems of aging, including disease and disability. A number of myths about aging began to form in the fabric of our culture. And over time, people accepted these myths as fact. What we need is to get above the clouds and catch a new view.

The boomers are going to demand that we look at aging differently. This is a generation of individuals who have never sat by passively and accepted the status quo. They have always been about change and doing things differently, and they are approaching the second half of life with this same fervor.

If we are serious about unleashing boomers for significant Kingdom impact, we have to change our view of aging. What if we simply decided to get above the clouds and began to see aging as something good and desirable, with potential and possibility? What if we began to view our own aging in a positive light rather than something to dread and avoid? There is no time like the present to make this shift in perspective. Go ahead and lift your head above what you currently know and catch a vision of what could be.

# Part Two

# THE
# BOOMER-AND-BEYOND
# WORLD

# 3

# AGING WELL

Sometimes when speaking to a group, I'll ask the audience, "What do you fear about getting older?" It's not unusual to hear answers like "Losing my memory," "Being dependent on someone else," or "Having no purpose." Heavy stuff—and all issues that are on the minds of most baby boomers. And rightly so.

Many boomers today are taking care of aging parents and are seeing firsthand what it is like to experience frailty, memory problems, and a loss of independence. Add to that the overwhelmingly high emphasis in our world on staying young, and you have a generation of people who will do nearly anything to maintain their health and vitality.

This desire has fueled the advent of things like Botox, herbal supplements, skin creams, and fitness centers. People spend billions of dollars every year in their quest to stay young and age well.

What it means to age well or age successfully is not of interest only to baby boomers; it is on the minds of people in their seventies, eighties, and nineties too. In fact, it may even enter the thoughts of young people. When we see an energetic eighty-four-year-old marathon runner on the news, followed by images of wheelchair-bound men and women living in nursing homes, we all tend to ask the question, "What can I do to one day have a life like the marathon runner's?"

Groundbreaking research conducted by the MacArthur foundation in the late 1980s and early 1990s identified three pillars for successful aging. And even though their initial research is nearly twenty years old, it continues to provide some of the leading information on successful aging. The three pillars for aging well are avoiding disease and disability, maintaining physical and mental function, and being actively engaged with life.[1]

To have effective ministry with this age group, we must understand these three components of successful aging and especially how these characteristics can be woven into the fabric of someone's walk with God.

## Maintaining Physical Health

Aging is inevitable, but frailty and disability are not. Heart attack, stroke, diabetes, cancer, and memory loss were once thought to be unavoidable ailments that came with age. But research demonstrates that lifestyle choices can play a huge role in healthy aging. A recent study reported that "elderly people who have a positive outlook, lower stress levels, moderate alcohol consumption, abstention from tobacco, moderate to higher income, and no chronic health conditions are more likely to thrive in their old age."[2] In a moment, we'll discuss some of these lifestyle choices and how the church can help promote good habits among people, but first we need to gain an understanding of the normal changes that occur with aging. I'm not talking about disease but rather about biological changes that are simply part of the natural aging process.

The first of the physical changes that just about everyone can expect is that our five senses tend to decline. As we get older, we don't see or hear quite as well as we used to. Sometime in the early to mid-forties, all of us develop presbyopia, which simply means "aging eye," and its main symptom is that we have to hold written material farther away from our faces in order to read it. It's correctable with glasses and doesn't pose any real limitations on our lives. The same is true for hearing. We hear best when we are young; this doesn't mean that everyone over fifty needs a hearing aid, but our hearing does weaken. Our sense of taste, touch, and smell also diminish, and yet these changes don't usually affect our quality of life.

The second typical sign of aging is that muscle mass and lung capacity both decline. A human being reaches a physical peak in the young adult years, roughly between the ages of 20 and 35. This is when athletes tend to perform best and when physical strength is at its greatest.

A few years ago, when my parents were visiting from out of town, my husband, Jon, and I drove them to see the new campus our church was building. It was especially muddy on the property, and our car got stuck. Both my dad and Jon got out of the car and started pushing. They were finally able to get it loose, and we drove home. I was intrigued by my father's heavy panting during the ride home, indicating how greatly he had exerted himself to get the car free. In contrast, my thirty-something husband made no sounds of distress. He was breathing quite normally. While my dad, in his sixties, is in great health, regularly walks eighteen holes on the golf course, and mows his own yard, it was clear that his lung capacity was less than Jon's.

Another typical change is that skin becomes less elastic. Skin isn't as tight as it once was, and wrinkles begin to appear. Our body also doesn't regulate temperature as well because of a loss of fatty tissue below the skin that helps insulate the body. I can still remember visiting my grandma and grandpa at Christmastime and seeing all my aunts and uncles wearing short-sleeved shirts despite the snow outside. It was because the heat was turned up for my grandparents. Only later did I learn that their need for more warmth was a normal part of aging.

For women, menopause signals the end of reproduction and a major marker of age. This can be a time of soul-searching for women who have found their purpose and identity through their children.

Finally, as we age, almost all of our organ systems gradually decline in function. Kidneys, heart, liver, sexual organs— everything begins to slow down. Nancy Hooyman and Asuman

Kiyak report that on average, many of our organ systems show a decline of about 1 percent per year after age thirty.[3]

My purpose for listing some of these physical changes is not to fill us with dread but to remind us that aging has always been a part of God's plan. Once Adam and Eve sinned in the garden, we became mortal beings, people who would not live in these physical bodies forever. In fact, our bodies are described in Scripture as tents (2 Corinthians 5:1; 2 Peter 1:13)—temporary shelters. Aging is God's way of moving us from birth to death and then to eternity. Aging is not to be feared or avoided. In fact, God sees it as a blessed time of life:

> "You [Abram], however, will go to your fathers in peace and be buried at a *good* old age." (Genesis 15:15; emphasis added)

> "Gray hair is a crown of splendor; it is attained by a righteous life." (Proverbs 16:31)

> "Even to your old age and gray hairs I am He, I am He who will sustain you. I have made you and I will carry you; I will sustain you and I will rescue you." (Isaiah 46:4)

> "The glory of young men is their strength, gray hair the splendor of the old." (Proverbs 20:29)

The world has produced a distorted view of aging in which youth is glorified and put on a pedestal. Through television, print media, movies, and advertising, we are bombarded with the message that "younger is better." We fear death and often fail to accept the body's natural decline.

For years, scientists and researchers have been seeking to discover why the body ages and if there is anything we can do about it. One of these researchers, Leonard Hayflick, attempted to explain aging by analyzing human cells. He found that our cells have a limited capacity for doubling. In other words, our cells will eventually no longer produce new cells. This study confirms what Scripture teaches: that life is finite. We are not meant to live forever. God has numbered our days, and He alone sustains each of our lives.

With that said, should we encourage people to do anything about their own aging? What about lifestyle habits that could be changed? Many of the debilitating problems of old age occur because of chronic illness, *not* because of the normal physical changes I mentioned earlier. Certainly, our risk for developing diseases increases as we age, but most of these can be postponed or perhaps even avoided by taking good care of the body.

## Keys to Healthy Aging

For quite some time now, research has repeatedly confirmed that certain lifestyle choices lead to better health and reduced frailty. Most of these are practically instinctive: good nutrition (eating whole grains, fruits, and vegetables), exercise, maintaining a healthy weight, not smoking, and having regular doctor visits all contribute to aging well.

Consider just a few outcomes from some recent studies:

- In a study involving nearly ten thousand women, those who exercised regularly were less likely to develop breast cancer than those who got little physical activity.[4]
- Adults who get very little physical activity are 80 percent more likely to develop heart disease than very active people.[5]
- Smoking causes lung cancer, but when an otherwise healthy individual quits smoking, the risk of developing lung cancer drops significantly. In fact, fifteen years after quitting, the risk of lung cancer is almost as low as if the person had never smoked at all.[6]
- Individuals whose diets are low in calcium are at a greater risk for developing osteoporosis.
- Two-thirds of all deaths are due to diseases associated with poor diets and dietary habits.[7]

When people choose to engage in healthy behaviors, such as eating right and regular exercise, there will be obvious physical benefits. Through the encouragement of their doctor, the media, or family members, many older adults are making the choice to alter their lifestyle in order to improve their health. Others, however, are still not convinced that a healthy lifestyle will truly make a difference in their own successful aging.

Whether people are motivated to improve their health or haven't given it much thought, issues of physical health will have to be addressed in order to effectively minister with boomers. The challenge for us is to help people discover a balance between completely ignoring their health and going overboard and obsessing about it. The bottom line is that we want to lead people to be good stewards of the body God has given them.

## A God-Centered View of Health

In my limited study of Scripture, I fail to find any place where God explicitly states that we are never to touch a cheeseburger or we must spend forty-five minutes on the treadmill each day. However, the Bible is clear that our bodies are not our own but belong to Him. "Do you not know that your body is a temple of the Holy Spirit, who is in you, whom you have received from God? You are not your own; you were bought at a price. Therefore honor God with your body" (1 Corinthians 6:19–20).

Honoring God always starts with putting Him first. Period. The motivation for keeping the body healthy and in top condition should be about pleasing Him and keeping ourselves fit in order to best serve Him for as long as He desires. It's not about having people shower us with compliments about how young we look or to take pride in outperforming our peers in physical endeavors. The goal is to make good and wise decisions regarding our bodies so that we can give God our best.

Beginning to address this topic of successful aging from a God-centered perspective communicates to the boomers in your church that you care about one of the primary issues on their minds. Just as teenagers are preoccupied with thoughts about peer pressure, college choices, and dating relationships, older adults are bombarded every day with the fact that they are aging. There are a variety of ways leaders can encourage healthy habits while helping people keep their central focus on God.

One of the first things that can be done is to host a health fair on the church campus. Health fairs function to connect people in the community with services that are available. Typically, community agencies like hospice, the Alzheimer's Association, grief support groups, and home health providers, along with many others, are willing to set up a booth in order to educate people about their services and help them with their needs. It is not unusual for blood pressure screenings, legal information, and nutritional counseling to be provided at these fairs. Although it does take some organization, the cost to a church is minimal as these providers are generally eager for opportunities to tell others about their services. This type of event communicates compassion to people both in the church and on the outside.

You can also encourage small groups to form around particular interests in exercise. I know of a number of churches that have biking groups. People meet regularly for rides and feel comfortable inviting non-Christians. One such group in Colorado has seen an older adult come to Christ and become an active part of the church as a result of the relationships he formed on various bike rides. Other churches have hiking groups, walking clubs, and exercise classes. Some churches supply Scripture verses on cards for walking participants to memorize as they are exercising.

Another way that churches can be encouraging is to teach what the Bible says about physical health. The Bible speaks about the importance of self-discipline (2 Timothy 1:7). God wants us to learn to say no to sin and the things of the flesh and yes to the things of the Spirit. Helping people learn this through diet and exercise can equip them for harder and more serious spiritual decisions, such as making time each day to pray or resisting temptation. In addition, God wants to be our central focus. The emphasis on looking young and staying youthful can make exercise and healthy eating an obsession among people. When something, even good health practices, takes up tremendous amounts of time and mental energy, it can easily become an idol.

Exercise has been a challenge for me as an adult. I like to make excuses about it being too cold for me to walk outside or my being just too tired. I'd much rather sit in a chair and read a good book. A few years ago, we bought a cheap treadmill at a garage sale, and it has helped change my exercise routine. Now I look forward to my thirty-minute walk because I see it as my worship time. It has become my habit to listen to worship music and meditate on certain Scriptures as I'm walking. This has changed my outlook, and I eagerly anticipate the time I'm going to spend with God. My mental focus is on Him, not on how many calories I'm burning.

## Maintaining Mental Health

While being able to remain independent and physically capable is a priority for many aging adults, so is their desire to stay mentally fit. Jokes and stories abound about people having a "senior moment" and no longer being able to remember things of importance.

Many people assume that losing their memory is inevitable, but significant memory loss usually signals that something else is going on in the brain. Because this is one of the greatest fears that plagues boomers and older adults, I'm going to give you a quick overview of memory and aging so that you are better equipped to understand the concerns so many adults face.

*Dementia* is an umbrella term for the loss of mental functioning. Unfortunately, some doctors will still give a diagnosis of "senile dementia" to a patient, even though that doesn't really identify anything specific. *Senile* simply means "old." So theoretically, we have "senile" ears and "senile" knees in addition to a "senile" mind. Senile dementia comes from the myth that older people have memory problems simply because they are old. Research is beginning to show that this is simply not true. Even in the later years of life, the brain is capable of forming new memories and learning new things.

From a medical standpoint, there are two categories of dementia: reversible and irreversible. Reversible dementia includes memory loss that comes from medications, such as the side effects caused by the meds or from the interactions among a number of medications. Whenever someone comes to me worried about a drastic memory change in a loved one, my first suggestion is to bag up all the person's medicines and take them to a doctor or pharmacist. Often some simple readjustments in dosages or prescriptions will fix the problem. However, if we assume that the memory problem is a reflection of their age and don't ask for a review of the medications, such a simple reversal may never be realized.

Other reversible causes of memory loss include depression, poor nutrition, dehydration, fatigue, and grief. Reversible memory loss may also show up with certain medical conditions such as thyroid disorders or diabetes.

Irreversible dementia is caused from such things as Parkinson's disease, brain injuries, and some strokes. The most common irreversible dementia is Alzheimer's disease.

It is estimated that five million people have Alzheimer's,[8] which attacks the brain and affects memory, thinking, reasoning, and language skills. Despite the fact that a large number of studies are being conducted, there is still no cure for Alzheimer's, and scientists have not yet discovered its cause. Many boomers who are taking care of aging parents are experiencing firsthand the devastating effects of this disease, which is why boomers are so interested in what they can do to prevent it in themselves. A MetLife Foundation survey with one thousand adults age fifty-five and older found that older adults fear developing Alzheimer's disease more than any other illness.[9]

Taking care of the mind is similar to taking care of the physical body. God knows the plans He has for our individual lives, and there are no guarantees that certain behaviors will prevent Alzheimer's disease, but there are things people can do to stay mentally fit.

Learning something new is one of the most important things we can do for our mind. For too long, people have believed the myth that "you can't teach an old dog new tricks." When we force ourselves to learn something new, we make new neurological connections in the brain, which strengthens our minds. The Lifelong Learning Center was a ministry I implemented after evaluating several other churches that were conducting similar programs. One morning a week on our campus, we offered a variety of classes for retirees. Subjects included current events, writing your memoirs, defending your faith, and gardening tips. Most often the courses were taught by retirees who were experts in that particular field. Part of the day included a devotion and prayer time in order to point people to the ultimate Teacher. Not only did retirees from the church participate, but so did older adults from the surrounding neighborhoods.

Many colleges and universities have lifelong learning programs for older adults, and these courses are usually taught by professors and experts in the field. My seventy-six-year-old father-in-law has participated in these courses for a number of years and has studied art history, basic German, and music appreciation.

Traveling is another way to challenge the mind, especially if the travel is to places never visited before. Green Acres Baptist Church in Tyler, Texas, has created a ministry called Firm Foundations that combines travel and education in a way that permits adults to learn more about the history of the Christian faith. Typically, the church hosts classes for four to six weeks before the trip so that participants can learn about the region and also study topics from Christian history that relate to it. Tours have included "Christianity Behind the Wall," a trip to eastern Europe, and "America's Spiritual Heritage," a trip to Washington, D.C., and Virginia. The church also sponsored a trip to Europe that included a day spent refurbishing C. S. Lewis's home in Oxford, England.

Other suggestions for keeping the mind sharp include playing games, reading, taking up a new hobby, playing a musical instrument, and dancing. The real key to exercising the brain is to do things that are novel. Once we have completely mastered a subject or hobby, the benefits to the brain are not as strong.

And though we may be tired of hearing it, physical exercise actually contributes to better mental health. Aerobic exercise has the most positive effects because it increases blood flow to the brain, produces endorphins, and increases brain oxygen levels.

Although the church can develop programs and ministries to address these needs, the unique slant we bring into the culture is pointing people to God's Word and what He has to say about the mind. Many boomers and older adults are plagued by fear and worry, yet the Bible clearly states that we are to not worry (Matthew 6:25) because this reflects a lack of trust in God. Interestingly, worry and stress have a negative effect on brain wellness. So leading people to understand fear and worry as sin and equipping them to "take captive every thought to make it obedient to Christ" (2 Corinthians 10:5) should be our first priority in helping people be mentally fit.

To have a healthy mind, people must dwell on the things of God and trust Him. Of course, each individual has to make the decision to trust God completely. But we can help by teaching through sermons, Bible studies, and one-on-one conversations that God is indeed trustworthy. We can also share examples from our own lives of instances when God proved to be worthy of our trust.

A number of years ago, our family went through a difficult time of uncertainty. Broken trust by a loved one left me with a tremendous amount of anxiety regarding the future. During this time, I wrote out twenty Bible verses about trust and fear and peace on note cards. I kept them with me at all times, reading them over and over until they were memorized. One that impressed me the most was Isaiah 26:3: "You will keep in perfect peace Him whose mind is steadfast, because He trusts in you."

I thought to myself, "That is what I want—perfect peace. And the way to get it is to keep my mind completely steadfast on God, never turning away from His face." This verse became my constant companion. As soon as I would catch myself worrying, I would tell myself to bring my mind back to trusting God.

Trusting God means trusting His Word, and to renew the mind, God's Word must be fully embraced and used as a source of strength and hope.

## Staying Engaged with Life

The third component of successful aging described by Rowe and Kahn is being actively engaged with life. Their research identified having relationships and doing something productive as the two keys to living an engaged life.

For many people, these two factors are found through employment and family. Aging can bring about significant changes in both of these roles. Children grow up and move out of the house, greatly altering the role of parenting, and retirement causes many people to reevaluate what gives their life meaning and purpose.

Because these two issues are of such importance to boomers, I will devote the entire next chapter to the topic of relationships and two other chapters to the topics of retirement and service (both issues related to productivity).

Too often society underestimates the significance of these things. Older adults who have meaningful relationships are healthier and more satisfied with life. And the desire to feel productive is a deep need in all of us. In fact, I agree with a speaker whom I once heard who said that humans can live with great pain and suffering as long as they feel their lives have purpose. The dictionary defines *productive* as "generative," "creative," "producing abundantly," "fruitful." Some people feel that they are only productive if they are earning a paycheck, whereas others feel productive if they cook a delicious meal for their family or friends to enjoy.

Make no mistake, as we consider how to minister with the new old in the coming years, the issue of productivity must be in the forefront of our minds. Older adults are redefining what this means for their lives, and the church needs to step in to help write this new script.

Leading-edge boomers will expend themselves on something. If we don't engage them in productive and meaningful ministry, they will invest themselves elsewhere. Some may choose to spend their time on hobbies, travel, or part-time work. Regardless of what the activity is, they *will* search for something to fill their life with purpose.

We have a small window of opportunity, right now, to influence how these older boomers use their time, abilities, and talents. It is imperative that we not waste the chance to call them into a life of meaningful work and service. For as we do, we will demonstrate to society what productive, purposeful, and successful aging truly looks like.

## A Story of Successful Aging

For quite a while now, I've been fascinated with the story of two older people nestled in Luke 2. Right after the fanfare of Jesus' birth, we meet these two folks. I'm amazed that Luke spends such a significant amount of space (fourteen verses to be exact) writing about these people, Simeon and Anna. As I wrap up this chapter, I want us to focus specifically on what we can learn from Anna. In Luke 2:36–38, we discover quite a few facts about her. She was old. She was a widow. She worshiped, fasted, and prayed. She taught others about the Messiah.

I tend to believe she lived a very engaged life. Verse 37 specifically says she never left the temple. This could mean she actually lived at the temple, or it may mean she was there whenever the doors were open. Regardless, her life was one of devotion to God. She was constantly growing in her relationship with Him by worshiping Him, fasting, and praying. I would expect this kept her mentally sharp as she put her focus exactly where it needed to be: on her Lord. I also can't help but think that all those hours spent in the temple gave her the opportunity to be relationally involved in many lives. Every day, people were coming to the temple to offer sacrifices and to uphold the Jewish customs, and she was there. I imagine she encouraged, advised, and taught others about the things of God. And we know for sure that she was productive in that she "spoke about the child to all who were looking forward to the redemption of Jerusalem" (v. 38). Is there any greater purpose than that?

As a new generation of older adults begins to emerge, they are struggling to uncover what it means to age well. Our culture is telling them that successful aging means being active, having good health, and keeping a sharp mind, and people are scrambling to fill their lives with anything that promises to do these things. Some would rather die than face frailty or disability. And while there is nothing wrong with paying attention to these three successful aging components, true and lasting fulfillment and purpose don't come from being healthy or from staying young. In fact, there are no guarantees that anyone will live a long life just by exercising or doing crossword puzzles. The only sure guarantee of successful aging comes from a deep, abiding relationship with Jesus Christ. This is the hope we have to offer. And this is why ministry with this generation can no longer be ignored.

# 4

# RELATIONSHIPS AND RESPONSIBILITIES

One Sunday afternoon, I met Patty, a sixty-four-year-old woman who was visiting her mother at the retirement community where my husband is the chaplain. She was quickly reconnecting with a friend in the lobby before rushing off to take some items to her mother. In a few moments, I learned that she has three living siblings, but she is the primary caregiver for her mom. Her eighty-five-year-old mother was in the retirement community for a short rehabilitation after knee surgery, but even when she is at home, Patty is the person who provides for most of her needs. Patty takes her mom grocery shopping, helps with the laundry, and provides companionship and a listening ear.

Patty also mentioned that her grandchildren, ages thirteen and ten, have lived with her and her husband, Mike, since the children were very young. This arrangement began when their son and the children's mother divorced and he gained part-time custody. Unable to work a full-time job and care for the needs of the children, he moved in with his mother and father.

Patty and Mike have been married for forty-five years and work side by side as the owners and managers of several rental properties. They are active in their church, attending regularly and serving in various capacities. She was smiling and upbeat as I talked with her, though it was obvious she was very busy.

Patty's story is not unusual. Over the years, I've encountered many older adults who are attempting to juggle a variety of roles and responsibilities. Most older adults want to take an active part in the lives of their grandchildren, have a meaningful relationship with their spouse, be involved in the care of their aging parents, and continue to support and love their adult children. In fact, these relationships, as well as connections with friends and other family members, are among the top priorities for most boomers.

In 2006, the Yankelovich research group conducted a study with boomers and found that in terms of what they wanted to do in the coming years of their life, 80 percent planned to focus energy on their grandchildren and 77 percent said they planned to spend more time with their family.[1]

The joys and struggles many boomers are facing in these relationships presents a wide range of untapped ministry opportunities. But to create these ministries, we have to get a glimpse of what these relationships look like and how these relationship dynamics are affecting the day-to-day lives of older adults.

## Grandparenting

I've heard numerous grandparents express their sentiments about the role of grandparenting in these words: "If I knew how much fun being a grandparent was going to be, I would have had my grandchildren first!" Their faces light up nearly every time you mention their grandchildren.

It is estimated there are seventy to eighty million grandparents in the United States, with millions more living all over the world.[2] Half of all adults become grandparents before they reach the age of sixty.[3] People can potentially become a grandparent from their late thirties to one hundred years of age. There is great variation in terms of when someone becomes a grandparent, but there is no question that many adults in the fifty to seventy age range are completely immersed in this role.

Today's grandparents are vastly different from the grandparents of fifty years ago. Kathryn Zullo reflects on her own personal experience in A Boomer's Guide to Grandparenting, which she wrote with her husband:

I would wake up in my grandparents' farmhouse to the smell of fresh cinnamon rolls baking in the oven. In the afternoon I'd find a batch of Grandma's homemade cookies cooling on the rack. She made bread from scratch and picked vegetables from her garden. After a week at Grandma's, I would go home with a sweater that she had knit by hand. She had twenty-six grandchildren—and she made every one of them sweaters when they came to visit.

I adored my grandmother. I always thought everyone should have a grandma like mine. But I can't be like her. I don't bake cookies. I don't knit sweaters. I don't grow my own veggies. I don't have time, with all the work and travel I do. What kind of grandmother is that?[4]

A boomer grandparent may still work in a demanding career, spend time exercising at the gym, and have a variety of hobbies. I know one new grandfather who plays guitar in a band. Other grandparents may be involved in camping, refinishing furniture, or scrapbooking. Even if they are retired, their lives may be full with volunteer work, commitments with friends, and church activities. And although the grandparenting role is going to look different than it did in the past, we can be sure that the majority of today's grandparents will make this role one of their top priorities.

## Today's Grandparent

It appears that people of boomer age and older are willing to do almost anything for the sake of their grandchildren. For one thing, grandparents today will rearrange their schedules and make adjustments in their own lives to accommodate their grandchildren. We have friends in their early fifties who have recently experienced the birth of their first grandchild. They run their own business in which both of them work, yet when the baby was born, the grandma purchased a laptop computer in order to fulfill her work commitments away from the office. At a moment's notice, she could now step in and babysit or help with the grandchild. Her son told me that his mom has made it clear that she wants to babysit for this child anytime. He said, "If she had her way, she would be the primary babysitter!" I've met another grandma who traveled an hour and a half to her daughter's home every Sunday night and stayed until Friday in order to care for her two grandchildren while the mother worked at her dental practice.

Spending money on grandchildren is another growing phenomenon among grandparents. As a generation, boomers have been willing to splurge on new cars, bigger houses, and designer clothes throughout their lives. They have approached shopping and spending much differently from their parents, who were products of the Great Depression and tended to be savers. My maternal grandparents (born in 1903 and 1907) certainly liked to give to their grandchildren, but their gifts consisted of handmade mementos and perhaps a quarter to spend downtown. Today's grandparents are big spenders who tend to buy expensive toys and other big-ticket items that Mom and Dad won't buy—and industries are marketing to them.

Not long ago, older adults wanted to learn the computer so that they could use e-mail and stay connected with their grandchildren. This has grown to include great-grandparents as well as grandparents, who have accounts on Facebook and use text messaging to stay in step with the younger members of their family. And technology is not the only thing grandparents are willing to learn in order to forge relationships. Many grandparents are taking classes, watching certain television programs, and learning about the interests of their grandchildren, all in an attempt to stay relevant and enjoy a mutually satisfying relationship.

Bob and Pat try to attend most school events in which their grandchildren are participating. By traveling to football games, band concerts, and theater programs, they not only communicate love and support to each grandchild but also get to know the grandchild's friends and teachers. This enriches the relationship they have with their grandchildren and allows for more meaningful conversations simply because they better understand the people and circumstances of their grandchildren's world.

## Challenges in Grandparenting

Not everything about the grandparent role is easy. Many grandparents face major difficulties, and we can expect these challenges to continue to grow and affect people in our churches and communities.

One of these challenges is grandparents' having to assume the role of surrogate parent. Millions of American grandparents are the primary caregivers for their grandchildren. In some cases, the parents have died, are incarcerated, or are abusing drugs or alcohol. In other instances, the parents are simply unable or unwilling to take on the full-time responsibility of parenting, though they may be somewhat involved.

A married couple from my childhood church were in their mid-fifties when they were thrown into the surrogate parent role. Their youngest son and his girlfriend had a child in high school and attempted to care for the baby with both sets of grandparents babysitting frequently. When they had a second child, it became too much for the mother to handle, especially since she preferred a party-type lifestyle. She moved one hour away and left the children in the care of the grandparents. Over time, she moved out of state, and the paternal grandparents and their son went to court to obtain custody of the children. Off and on for a number of years, the grandchildren lived with the grandparents, who became the primary caregivers and shouldered the responsibility of disciplining the grandchildren, providing for their basic needs, meeting with their teachers at school, and involving them in extracurricular activities.

The surrogate parent role can put a tremendous amount of stress on grandparents. Some grandparent caregivers have health problems and struggle with depression. They experience guilt over the failures of their own son or daughter and at times may feel resentful about taking on the role of child rearing during a time in their life when they could be traveling more or pursuing their own interests and activities.

Another challenge for grandparents comes when their son or daughter divorces. This can create a web of complicated relationships. Some divorcing parents tend to divorce the spouse's family along with the spouse. The result is often that grandparents have little or no contact with their grandchildren, which can be heartbreaking for all the generations. As the divorce rate has climbed, laws have been passed to protect grandparents, giving them the right to petition courts for legal visitation privileges with their grandchildren. In other instances, divorce means that the grandparents step into a much more active role in helping both the single parent and the grandchildren. This can take the form of providing financial assistance, allowing the parent and children to live in the grandparents' home, or helping with day-to-day child care needs.

For many people, the grandparent-grandchild relationship is difficult to maintain simply because they do not live close to one another. It takes a greater effort on the part of the parents to help the older and younger generations connect. Regular phone calls, sending notes and gifts through the mail, and scheduled visits are just a few of the things that can help relationship ties form across the miles. Advancements in technology also have helped improve long-distance relationships. Using a camera designed for the computer and software such as Skype, grandparents and grandchildren can now see each other on the computer screen when they call. This enables the grandchildren to explain artwork they've done at school or even show off the new way they've arranged their bedroom.

## Ministry with Grandparents

As we attempt to get inside the world of aging adults, we must recognize how important the role of grandparenting is to most of these people. Churches should not ignore the time, money, and energy spent on this particular relationship. Because leading-edge boomers are taking this role so seriously, it can be a primary way to reach out to people in the community as well as those in the church.

We know boomers are looking for ways to establish meaningful connections with their grandchildren; therefore, churches and denominations may want to consider hosting grandparent-grandchild retreats. Activities might include swimming, canoeing, hayrides, cookouts, and crafts. Spiritual teaching that applies to both generations would enhance the time spent together.

Exploritas, formerly named Elderhostel, is an educational organization that promotes lifelong learning among older adults. It offers a wide variety of educational programs, some of the most popular being travel and learning experiences specifically for grandparents and grandchildren. A Daniel Boone experience in Kentucky, a ski adventure in the Rockies, and a Yellowstone National Park trip are just a few of many tours planned for grandparents and grandchildren. Grandparents can get to know their grandchildren better when they spend time away, having a shared experience.

Dave is a sixty-six-year-old man in our community who is passionate about mentoring men to become strong spiritual leaders. He invests in the men in his own family by spending large amounts of time with each of them. Recently, his four sons and the five oldest grandsons, ranging in age from eight to sixteen, went on a seven-day fishing trip to Canada. Dave believes that boys learn a great deal about what it means to be godly men through observation and hands-on experience in activities such as this.

Mission trips or service opportunities specifically designed for grandparents and grandchildren can also provide a unique bonding experience. One sixty-three-year-old grandfather took two of his teenage grandsons on an eighteen-day mission trip. They traveled to a number of Southeast Asian countries, smuggling Bibles and bringing money as gifts. They met with Christians in each country to talk with them, provide encouragement, and in some cases share devotions. Most important, the grandfather was able to help his grandsons gain a different perspective on life and learn to appreciate the opportunities they have available to them in America. Whether it is an overseas mission trip or a project in your local community, the experience of serving together is especially valuable.

Another way churches can minister to grandparents is through a grandparenting conference. First Evangelical Free Church in Fullerton, California, held a two-day conference for grandparents that included speakers discussing such topics as the responsibilities of grandparenting and the difficult situations grandparents in dysfunctional families face. In addition to the speakers, the conference included worship, reflection, discussion, and lunch. The first day was devoted to the formal conference, and the second day featured a trip to the local zoo for grandparents and their grandchildren. This provided an immediate way for grandparents to enjoy their grandchildren and even practice some of what they had learned during the teaching sessions.

Churches can also serve grandparents by coaching them on how to leave a spiritual legacy for their grandchildren. Spending time and money on grandchildren seems to be what new grandparents are doing to influence their grandchildren. But in the long run, it is most important for these young people to be positively affected by their grandparents' Christian faith. Second Timothy 1:5 reminds us that Timothy's grandmother and mother were both sincere believers in Christ who modeled this to Timothy.

Bob and Pat, whom I mentioned earlier, are grandparents who strive to pass on a spiritual legacy to their grandchildren.

One way they do this is by taking a few moments at the annual family Christmas gathering to share their values and things important to them. For example, one year they talked about the important decision of choosing a mate. They reminded the grandchildren to focus on more than appearance or money and instead look for someone who cares about his or her spiritual life and will remain committed to the relationship until the end of life. The sharing time is relatively short and usually occurs immediately after the gifts have been opened. One year, Bob and Pat were able to give each grandchild a sizable financial gift, and in doing this, they told them, "We believe in you and consider you our best investment." Bob and Pat have taken grandchildren to see the places their grandparents were baptized and have told the youngsters about their decisions to follow Christ. Interestingly, Bob was motivated to begin leaving a spiritual legacy after hearing a woman speak about the legacy her own grandfather left her. Sometimes a church simply needs to mention these suggestions in a sermon or a Bible study to prod people to do more in their grandchildren's lives.

Another way grandparents can leave a spiritual legacy is by sending a birthday card to each grandchild on his or her spiritual birthday—the anniversary of the day the young person gave his or her life to Christ. Grandparents can offer love and encouragement through this yearly remembrance.

Churches can help older adults pass on their legacy by hosting activities specifically for grandchildren and their grandparents. These events could take the form of a dinner with a Christian magician, a special brunch with a program, or even a hike and picnic. While these events should include something fun, it is important to provide faith-related questions at the event and to allot time for the grandparents and grandchildren to talk one-on-one using the discussion starters. The conversation starters might include "Tell me about your earliest faith experience," "What is one of your favorite verses in the Bible and why?" "What is your favorite Bible story or Bible character and why?" or "When was a time God answered one of your prayers?" Older adults and children who do not live close to their grandparents or grandchildren should not be excluded from these events; rather, an older adult could "adopt" a young person and vice versa.

Sheryl is a woman in our church who regularly invites our daughter, Ella, to her house to eat dinner and play while my husband and I go out on a date. Sheryl gives Ella birthday and Christmas presents and takes a genuine interest in her life. When it was grandparents' day at Ella's preschool, her grandparents were unable to make the long trip to attend, but Sheryl was more than willing to be a stand-in grandma, participating in all the activities and even taking pictures. Churches should encourage the formation of these relationships, as it is good for both children and older adults to know that they are loved and valued even beyond their own family. We can help make these relationships happen by inviting older adults to serve in the children and youth ministries and by promoting intergenerational small groups and classes.

Churches can also support grandparents who do not live near their grandchildren by providing a resource that lists suggestions for long-distance grandparenting. This could be a handout available in the church lobby or a page on the church Web site. Long-distance grandparents can be encouraged to record stories about their lives and send these to the children in the mail. Grandparents and grandchildren might choose the same book to read and set a time to discuss the book on the telephone. They also could pick the same Bible verse to memorize.

While grandparenting is very important to aging boomers, it is not the only relationship affecting the lives of older adults. The relationship boomers have with their adult children can in fact be intertwined with the grandparent-grandchild relationship.

## Adult Children

There is great diversity in the types of relationships adults have with their adult children, but a few trends are emerging.

"Helicopter parent" is a term used to describe parents who hover over their children even after the children have left the nest. You'll find the term used most often in higher education because many parents attempt to manage the grades, finances, and friends of their college-age children. This has become such a big issue that 70 percent of universities and colleges have hired a parent coordinator who regularly interacts with parents and answers their questions.[5] Boomers have historically been more involved than any previous generation in managing their children's lives, seen in everything from the growth of day care centers to soccer teams and parent-teacher associations. This doesn't mean that all boomer parents spent lots of time with their children, but as a whole, they did manage and orchestrate many of their children's activities.

Sometimes this helicopter parenting style continues well past the college years and can create conflict in the parent–adult child relationship. Boomers may need help accepting that their children may marry someone they would not have chosen or pursue a career they themselves wouldn't like or are not driven as strongly as they were to make a lot of money. Tensions may be especially high over how the adult child parents their grandchildren.

Another interesting phenomenon occurring more often today is adult children moving back into the home of their parents. These adult children, often referred to as "boomerangs," usually return home for financial reasons, sometimes trying to save money in order to buy their own home or to pay off college loans. How well this arrangement works depends on whether the child has a job, shoulders some of the household responsibilities, and agrees to move out by a certain time.

Despite the challenges, most aging adults and their adult children enjoy a close relationship. They are willing to provide both physical and emotional support for one another, and the majority talk by phone or in person frequently. Both generations think about one another and worry about each other's lives. Adult children tend to be concerned about their parents' health, while aging parents may worry about a range of issues, including the adult children's health, safety, finances, and relationships.

I was reminded of this at a conference where I visited with an eighty-year-old man. He told me about his sixty-year-old son who had lost his job under trying circumstances. The whole ordeal had been difficult, resulting in depression and challenges as the son looked for work. It was obvious to me how sad and concerned this father was, and it reminded me of the cliché "once a parent, always a parent." Parents—even aging parents—do not stop loving or caring about their children.

## Reaching Out to Parents of Adult Children

Churches can help parents of adult children by applying sermons and Bible study lessons to relationship issues. It's helpful to teach parents how to use good listening skills when interacting with their children. It is also valuable to have discussions in a Sunday school class or a small group about how to share advice with one's adult children without putting them down. This can happen as a group of people reflect on what it was like when they were their children's age. How did they want to be treated by their parents? What would have been most helpful?

When I was pregnant with our daughter, I worried about her well-being and whether she would be born healthy. After listening to my concerns, my mom said she felt the same way when she was expecting me. She went on to say that during this particular period, she heard a sermon on Romans 8:28, "And we know that in all things God works for the good of those who love Him, who have been called according to His purpose." She said that at that moment, she made a conscious decision to trust God and believe in His purposes as she anticipated my arrival. My mother didn't preach at me or tell me I shouldn't be worrying; rather, she gave an example from her own life and left the rest up to the Holy Spirit. Some adults don't know how to communicate with their children in this way. Small groups in which real-life situations can be discussed and even practiced are beneficial.

Many churches have programs specifically designed to offer support to mothers of preschoolers. There are weekend conferences planned for parents and teenagers to address difficult issues related to the adolescent years. Why, then, would adults not benefit from opportunities to grow in their role as parents of adult children? No matter what the stage of life, people need the chance to interact with others so that they can openly share the relationship struggles in their lives and learn ways of applying biblical solutions to these problems. The parenting of adult children is just one more opportunity for God to help people become more like Him.

## Aging Parents

We've already identified the sixty-five-and-over age group as the fastest-growing segment of the population. But did you know within this group, adults who are eighty-five-and-over are growing even more rapidly? In fact, the eighty-five-plus population is expected to increase from 5.7 million in 2010 to 6.6 million in 2020.[6] People are living longer both in America and abroad, and many boomers are shouldering the responsibility of providing care for an elderly parent.

An overwhelming amount of time and attention is focused on this task. Most often the bulk of responsibility falls on a daughter (often the oldest), although there are many sons who are active and involved in the caregiver role as well.

The type of care provided varies by each individual situation and the specific circumstances. For some boomers, the aging parent has moved into their home and they are providing physical care, preparing meals, and managing finances. Others are actively involved in the care their parent is receiving in a nursing home or other long-term care setting. These caregivers make regular visits, do their parent's laundry, and act as an advocate for their parent. Some aging adults are still living in their own home but need assistance with everyday tasks. Adult children often make daily visits to help with cleaning, cooking, and chauffeuring them to their various appointments.

Caregiving is a demanding and stressful task that can be all-consuming. The "sandwich generation" is the name applied to middle-aged adults who are providing care for an aging parent and at the same time providing assistance to their own children, either children who are still living at home or adult children who are beginning their own families. Thus millions of boomers feel torn by the various needs they must fill within their family. And on top of the caregiving responsibilities, many of them are juggling the demands of their career or have been forced to leave their job in order to provide care.

In 2006, an AARP bulletin told the story of a fifty-eight-year-old woman who was giving a business speech when she received word not only that her elderly mother was in need of immediate medical attention but also that her pregnant daughter was in labor.[7] This is the type of situation in which many boomers find themselves. Balancing all of these demands creates a tremendous amount of stress.

When compared to the general population, caregivers have a greater risk of suffering from depression and using alcohol to deal with stress. Many struggle with feelings of guilt, sadness, anger, and resentment. They feel torn between the various people who need them.

What is most important in this context is thinking about some practical ways of serving caregivers inside and outside the church. One of the best ways we can minister to boomers is by tapping in to this need in their life.

## Ministry with the Caregiver

A great way to serve caregivers involves reaching out to their aging parent. Concerned sons or daughters will be looking for places where their parent can be involved in activities and will be loved and valued. Just as in the past boomers looked for churches with good children's and youth ministries, they will be pleased to find churches that will seek to love their parent as they do.

Council Road Baptist Church in Bethany, Oklahoma, designed an entire Sunday morning church service as well as other special programs throughout the day to honor World War II veterans. Some family members drove from out of state to attend the service with their parent. Other adult children were thrilled that their fathers were being honored. In a society where the aged are often forgotten, this program showed aging boomers and the community at large that this particular church values the legacy of older adults.[8]

A second suggestion is to provide services that offer caregivers a break from their caregiving duties. Caregivers need to be able to leave their caregiving responsibilities for a short time in order to attend to personal needs or simply to have a cup of coffee with a friend. Most communities have businesses whose primary purpose is to provide companionship for an older person while the caregiver leaves the home. However, these services charge an hourly rate. Church volunteers who are willing and available to spend a few hours a week with an aging person, at no cost, can be a tremendous blessing to worn-out caregivers.

A number of churches in Houston, Texas, have partnered to minister to individuals in the early stages of Alzheimer's disease. This program, called The Gathering, is an adult day care for people in the mild to moderate stages of Alzheimer's. Churches usually host The Gathering once a month, with as many as thirty churches throughout the city of Houston participating. This means that caregivers, if they so choose, can make use of day care at a different church throughout the city almost every day of the month. The Gathering typically gives caregivers a three-hour break from the constant demands of caring for their loved ones. There is no charge for the service. The individual with Alzheimer's is ministered to by volunteers who provide entertainment, read Scripture, tell jokes lead chair exercises, and serve a hot lunch.

Chapelwood United Methodist Church in Houston is one of the churches that hosts The Gathering. This church has taken the ministry a step further by offering a support group for the caregivers while their loved one attends The Gathering. Support groups are a third way for churches to minister to caregivers. These groups give caregivers a chance to process issues, share concerns, and offer encouragement to others who are in a similar life situation.

Online discussion forums and chat rooms for caregivers are growing in popularity because many caregivers are simply too busy to attend group meetings in person. These online groups allow people to post questions and have other caregivers and community experts respond with suggestions. Groups of this nature with a biblical perspective would be well received by many boomers.

People often turn to a church during times of crisis, and the trials of caregiving are no exception. When I was serving as the minister with adults fifty and over in the local church, I frequently had phone calls and meetings with people who needed to make decisions regarding the care of a loved one. Issues ranged from how to choose a nursing home and where to find home health services to how to handle the person's legal and financial affairs. I made it a priority to join organizations that served older adults in the community so that I would be aware of the variety of services available and have face-to-face contact with the service providers. In turn, I was able to envision ways our church could partner with the service providers in helping older adults in the community. If we were having a special program for the frail elderly or their caregivers, for example, I alerted these groups.

Churches can have a far-reaching impact in their community if they become clearinghouses for community resources. Caregivers do not have time to search the Internet for answers or wait on the line for their call to be received. A listening ear, coupled with brochures and phone numbers of reputable community services, is a blessing for many caregivers.

This can be especially helpful for children who do not live in the same community as their parents. Long-distance caregiving has some unique challenges, and adult children will appreciate a local church that can help them locate the appropriate resources.

A final suggestion is to help boomers have meaningful conversations with their parents. In the wake of a stroke, Alzheimer's disease, or other chronic illness, communication can be difficult. All of us want to have some special moments with our loved ones, but we aren't sure how to make this happen.

I have found reminiscing to be one of the best ways to bring about positive communication between the generations. Adult children usually enjoy hearing about their parents' past experiences, and older adults typically find pleasure in the sharing process. Research has also demonstrated that reflecting on the past is a healthy activity for the elderly. As we age, we need opportunities to process our lives and tell our stories.

A number of churches today are providing people with printed booklets full of questions that guide older adults in the reflection process. Some of the questions are "What was school like for you as a child?" "What did your dad or mom do for a living?" "How did you meet your spouse?" and "What did you do on dates?"

Often an adult child sits down with a parent, asking questions like these from the past and then writing out the answers or even recording them on audio or video to preserve them for future generations. I've had adult children tell me that this experience moved them deeply and that they discovered things about their parent they never knew. For example, one daughter was shocked to hear about the conditions her mother lived in during World War II when she and her husband were traveling. "My mother was forced to grow up at a very young age!"

Aging parents, in turn, feel valued when someone takes the time to listen to their stories, and the process of recalling past experiences may help them discover how meaningful their life has been.

It's important for us to recognize that not every adult child has embraced the caregiver role. Some choose to withdraw from their aging parent in an attempt to deny the aging process or even avoid their own thoughts of mortality. Others never received good counsel enabling them to work through strained or abusive relationships. While the majority of older adults do receive regular contact and care from their children, there are those who don't. Sound biblical teaching and encouragement on what it means to "honor your mother and father" and "care for the widow" may be all some families need to move into a more active and honoring role. Others need assistance to forgive past griev-ances and move toward healing and reconciliation. Helping people mend these relationships can be hard and messy work, but it is no doubt a privilege to enter into God's work of restoring broken relationships and ultimately leading people to Him.

## Siblings

The relationship between siblings is often overlooked, but as a person ages, this is a bond that grows in importance. As children, brothers and sisters tend to be close. But during the years of mar-riage, child rearing, and jobs, there is not enough time to con-tinue to build these relationships. Not to mention that as adults, siblings may live far apart and have few common interests.

Children leaving home, retirement, and the death of a spouse are all events that can bring siblings close together again. The contact between brothers and sisters may also grow as they work together to make decisions regarding the care of their aging parents. Sometimes conflict can develop between the adult chil-dren regarding who provides the care and in what manner it is given. The primary caregiver may feel resentful of the sister or brother who lives away and visits the parent only a few times a year. On the other hand, working together as caregivers or grieving the loss of parents can actually bring siblings even closer.

I've observed older siblings who take vacations together, talk daily on the phone, and even move from their homes in order to be close to one another. Living across the street from us is a sister and brother who are in their late seventies. Both of them have experienced the loss of their spouses and are meticulously trying to manage their finances. The sister bought the home, but her brother contributes to the arrangement by mowing the yard and working part time. They are able to provide practical help for each other as well as emotional support.

## Marriage Relationship

We can't leave this discussion of the important relationships in the life of an older adult without highlighting the marital bond. The marriage relationship is a highly complex and intimate relationship that changes as people age. Research has shown that marital satisfaction can be represented by a U-shaped curve. People tend to be happiest in the early years of married life, and then satisfaction declines in the middle years as the responsibilities of child rearing leave the couple with less time to focus on each other. If a couple navigate successfully through this time, they report high marital satisfaction again in the later years of life.

Interestingly, just as a healthy diet and exercise contribute to aging well, so does a strong marriage. People who have worked through their differences and remained together tend to be healthier in their older years than their single counterparts.

The church faces some definite changes in terms of marriage among aging baby boomers when compared with the builder generation that came before. The prevalence of divorce began to rise among the boomer generation, and many aging boomers may be single or in a second or third marriage.

The builder generation has been less likely to divorce, and some have stayed in unhappy marriages simply for the sake of commitment. Boomers, by contrast, have been more willing to divorce if they are not happy or their needs are not being met. In fact, Ken Dychtwald, a gerontology expert, says that as the boomers age, many of them may choose different life partners to coincide with their new interests.[9]

As church leaders, we must not make the mistake of assuming that because people are older, they have this marriage thing all figured out. Some folks do, and they can serve as great mentors and teachers, but other couples may need marital help and biblical guidance.

There are unquestionably some difficult life situations that can challenge the marriage relationship. Retirement is a major life transition that affects couples in late life. Seemingly overnight, a couple's daily routine changes as one or both partners are now at home more. Couples may need help redefining roles, such as who is going to do the housework and the shopping. They often need to work together to plan out the dreams and goals they have for this particular season of their life. Small group discussions, perhaps in conjunction with a Bible study, can help couples navigate these issues.

Children leaving home can also affect the marital relationship. If the marriage revolved around the activities and needs of the children, the couple should take time to get reacquainted and redefine what is important to them. There has been more talk in recent years about marriages that dissolve when children move out of the house. Some couples have stayed together "for the sake of the children" and may divorce at this time. It is crucial that the church step in to provide support, enrichment, and counseling during this time of transition. Pastors who plan a sermon series on marriage should not neglect to include a message or two discussing the uniqueness of the empty-nest marriage.

Caring for aging parents can also put strain on a marriage. Fully 89 percent of the respondents in an online survey by

Caring.com said that caring for an aging parent forced them to spend less time with their spouse, and 48 percent said that caregiving was causing them to feel less connected and attached to their partner.[10] For some partners, their dreams of spending more one-on-one time together after the children have left home are dashed because there is now a parent needing care.

One final pressure on marriages in late life is illness. When one spouse suffers from a chronic illness that affects quality of life, the marriage can suffer.

The support a church offers in terms of helping people care for an aging parent or assisting couples in the relationship with their adult children will also have positive benefits on the marriages of these individuals. Churches can also plan special activities that appeal to boomers and include a component of marriage enrichment in these activities. Dan Allen, minister to adults fifty-five-plus at McGregor Baptist Church in Fort Myers, Florida, hosted a five-day Caribbean cruise specifically for older boomer couples. As a part of the cruise, Dan and his wife, Blanche, included teaching and activities to strengthen the marriages of these couples. Dan said that many of these couples are in the throes of caring for an aging parent and may still have children at home, and this combination doesn't allow them much time to reconnect with each other and invest in the marriage relationship. The cruise was well received by these couples, as it not only provided needed relaxation but also time for growth.

## A Final Word

Although this chapter has focused on the family relationships of boomers, I don't want to end our discussion without mentioning the importance of friendships. Churches that are making intentional efforts to reach boomers are finding that it is important to provide opportunities for older adults to get together for fun. Whether it be a dinner out or an evening of music, this atmosphere helps boomers feel a sense of community with others in their same life stage. As they laugh together and enjoy one another, they will feel more comfortable talking about serious things, such as dealing with a wayward son or daughter or caring for a parent who has had a stroke.

Almost every time I ask older adults what brings meaning to their lives, relationships rank high on their list. When all is said and done, people are more important than how much money is in the portfolio or what travel excursion is being planned. As we age, we understand this better. This is absolutely true for the baby boomers. They are already devoting more time to relationships. Wise leaders will not ignore this but will recognize it as a way to connect and engage aging adults—both inside and outside the church.

# 5

# RETIREMENT

## What It Is and What It Is Becoming

From the time we are young, people start asking the question, "What are you going to be when you grow up?" The pressure of this question increases in intensity as one approaches graduation from high school and enters the college years. Now we hear, "What are you studying?" "What are you going to do after college?" And then throughout the first half of our adult life, conversations often begin with "So, tell me, what do you do?" or "How is work going?"

Then, somewhere around age fifty, give or take a few years, there is a shift and people begin to pose the question "When are you going to retire?"

The whole idea of working for a set number of years and then being retired for a number of years has become an accepted and even anticipated part of the life course. Young people are told to start putting money away for retirement while they are still in high school and in some cases even younger.[1] I've interacted with many college-age students who have retirement as their primary goal. Their plan is to work hard and then retire as soon as they can in order to enjoy life. One twenty-two-year-old said she looked forward to retirement as a "never-ending vacation."

In many ways, society has conditioned us to have this kind of mentality. When we get our first job, we are encouraged to start setting aside money for retirement. We are constantly inundated with messages demanding that we think about this season of our lives. For example, Social Security (and concern over Social Security) is a regular part of political conversation. People are encouraged to save on their own and not depend on Social Security alone to support them when they are older. Advertisements from the financial services industry bombard most of us on a daily basis, promising that a wealth-filled retirement full of leisure activities awaits all of us, but we must start planning for it now.

Retirement has become one of those cultural trends (like so many others) that Christians have simply accepted as normal. Find a job, get married, buy a house, have a baby, make money, and get ready to retire. Most of us have never questioned where this phenomenon of retirement came from, where it is headed, and most important of all, what God has to say about it.

Chapters Three and Four noted that aging boomers are highly concerned with keeping their bodies and minds young and are equally interested in investing in relationships. The third area that fills the thoughts of most boomers is the topic of retirement. Will I have enough money? Where should I live? What should I do with my time? If we want to better understand boomers and ultimately discover how to reach them with meaningful ministry, we must dive into the discussion of retirement.

## A Step Back in Time

The concept of retirement calls up the image of a person who is older, perhaps around the mid-sixties, who no longer works for money. It is a period of life when it is socially acceptable for someone to have abandoned a career. For example, we tend to think it is improper for a thirty-five-year-old to be not working, but it is perfectly fine for a sixty-five-year-old to be without work.

Retirement wasn't always viewed this way. In fact, retirement is a relatively new concept.

Before the Civil War, "retiring" meant you were going to bed or ducking indoors to wait out a storm; you expected to return to your labors a few hours later. At this time in history, most people had independent jobs as farmers and tradesmen. They worked hard to earn a living, and after paying for life's daily needs, there was little money left over for long-term savings. Older adults worked as long as their health would allow, and when illness and frailty forced them to stop working, life was usually difficult. Some may have had family, friends, and neighbors who provided for their needs, but others lived in a state of poverty and simply waited to die.

In the late 1800s and early 1900s, people began to have more industrialized jobs and were wage earners. This caused them to be dependent on the factory or company for whom they worked. Around this same time, retirement policies began to emerge, put in place primarily by business leaders who wanted to make room for younger workers because they believed that older workers were not as useful or as productive. Pensions became a part of some businesses, and yet many older workers still saw retirement as a threat. Retirement placed people at an economic disadvantage because they were making less money than before. Retiring also went against the American ideal that work was an important part of life.

During the Great Depression, both young and old found themselves without jobs. Poverty was common among people of all ages in all walks of life. In 1935, President Franklin Roosevelt signed the Social Security Act, which was designed, in part, to protect people from "old-age poverty." In other words, when Americans could no longer work because of frailty and disability associated with age, they would still have a partial income. The plan was originally developed to pay retirement benefits to the primary worker in a family, beginning at the age of sixty-five.

As the years went on, more and more adults were alive at age sixty-five and continued to live even further into their later years. They had to retire in order to receive Social Security benefits, and yet without work, many adults lived lives devoid of meaning. They were seen as having little social value and were often marginalized by society. Because of this, retirement was something to be dreaded. But sometime between 1950 and 1960, this attitude began to change.

Wise financial investment firms and some savvy business professionals began to see that a large group of discontented retirees presented a profitable business opportunity. Independent living communities for adults age fifty-five and over, such as Del Webb's Sun City and California's Leisure World, demonstrated that retirement could be a footloose and fancy-free time of life. Retirees were enticed to move to sunny locations like Florida and Arizona where they could spend their days golfing, lounging by the pool, or playing shuffleboard.

And even though many older adults preferred to not move but rather to stay close to family, the marketing of a carefree retirement lifestyle began to take hold. Retirement was viewed as a reward for a lifetime of hard work. It was common for workers to plan for and dream about a lifestyle of leisure once their years of work were completed.

This attitude became so mainstream that the concept of early retirement (retiring in one's fifties or early sixties) became popular. Adults worked hard and saved as much as they could in order to leave the labor force as quickly as possible. Just look at these statistics. Around the turn of the twentieth century, 65 percent of men age sixty-five and older were in the labor force. By 1950, 47 percent of men over sixty-five were still working.[2] But in 2008, only 21 percent remained in the workforce.[3]

Just as there was a shift in the perception of retirement as something to be dreaded to something to be pursued, the concept is once again being redefined, in large part because of the baby boomers.

## A Present-Day Look at Retirement

In early 2009, I talked with Jim, a man who had recently retired from his job as a nursing home administrator. It was hard to guess his age. He was in great shape physically and was obviously mentally sharp, as he was attending a continuing education workshop I was leading for health care professionals. I asked him over lunch why he chose to retire, and he explained that he had worked in the long-term care industry for many years. The job of a health care administrator is demanding and stressful and requires that you be available twenty-four hours a day, seven days a week. As our conversation progressed, he told me that his wife of thirty-four years had died nine years earlier of leukemia and that in recent years he had forged a new relationship with a woman who lost her life to melanoma.

These losses caused him to reflect on how he wanted to spend his remaining years, and so he chose to let go of the responsibilities of his demanding career. At the age of sixty-three, he retired and is now working fifteen to twenty hours a week managing a retirement apartment complex and fitness center. The job is flexible—which was important to him—because he enjoys traveling to visit his son in Florida and his daughter in Iowa. He noted that he has many interests to keep him busy, including running in marathons all over the country, enjoying the large piece of land he lives on, and spending time with his granddaughter.

The way in which he has carved out his retirement life reflects the desire of many adults in their fifties, sixties, and seventies. The New Retirement Survey, conducted by Merrill Lynch, revealed some interesting findings about how baby boomers are approaching retirement. Seventy-six percent of boomers want to keep working in retirement, but they would like to retire from their current job at around age sixty-four and launch into a new job or career.[4] Sometimes these are part-time jobs or jobs that allow flexibility, while others start a new full-time career. The types of jobs boomers are moving into include starting their own businesses, working in the nonprofit sector, or finding a fun job that is less stressful than their career job.

Ronnie owned and managed two oil and lube centers in Louisiana before selling his business and retiring at the age of fifty-five. He wanted more time to spend with his grandchildren and to be available to provide care for his aging parents. After a few years of "full-time retirement," he wanted to do some part-time work and decided to start a car wash business. One of the primary reasons he continues to work is because of his desire to interact with nonbelievers. He told me, "If I didn't have this job, I would spend 90 percent of my time with other Christians, volunteering at church and participating in church-related activities."

He loves to hire young people as employees and then look for opportunities to talk with them about a relationship with the Lord. He said to me, "Spiritual conversations come up naturally as you take time to genuinely care about people and their needs." Not only is he able to influence his employees, but he also cares about the customers. He listens to the concerns people have, points them to resources that could help them, and commits to pray for them.

Ronnie's postretirement job not only gives him the chance to minister "on the job" but also gives him the flexibility to participate in mission trips. Ronnie went on his first mission trip at the age of fifty-five (shortly after retiring from his full-time career), and now, at the age of sixty-five, he has been on ten or eleven mission trips, including six trips to Africa.

Boomers, like Ronnie, are choosing to continue to work in their lifelong career or a new postretirement job. Some are working for the additional income, while others work for personal satisfaction and to stay mentally challenged. For those choosing a new career path in retirement, the New Face of Work Survey discovered that half of adults age fifty to seventy want their work to benefit the community and people in need. The jobs they are interested in include working to help the poor, the elderly, and the disenfranchised of society. Others are interested in working in health care, education, civic activism, arts and culture, and the environment.[5]

## The Future of Retirement

A future retirement trend that is just beginning to take shape is the idea of a cyclic rather than a linear life cycle.[6] For years, our lives have been set up in a linear fashion: get an education in the early years, work hard in the middle years, and pursue leisure in the later years. The new generation of older adults is beginning to blur the lines of this linear approach to life. A cyclic approach to life means that boomers may retire from their current job and spend a year or two traveling and enjoying leisure activities, then go back to college or pursue a different career. Work, education, and leisure are woven in and out of the life course.

Many boomers want to scale back from their demanding careers and have a more flexible lifestyle. They want to be able to work at a job they enjoy, but on their own time schedule. They don't want to punch a clock or feel tied down. Boomers place high importance on having freedom to do the things they want to do, such as travel, engage in hobbies, or visit family. They also want time for educational interests that will not only enrich their lives but also help them in the new jobs they want to pursue.

Robert Butler, one of the founding fathers of gerontology, suggests that our lives should include periodic retirements, rather than saving up all of our retirement for the later years of life. He says:

> Would we not be better served by replacing the three tight compartments of education, work, and retirement that evolved in modern times with an interweaving of all three throughout life to avoid programmed obsolescence? That would ensure an up-to-date, knowledgeable, and efficient workforce and reduce the fear that an aging workforce must inevitably result in economic stagnation. These changes in education, work, and retirement would help women who, because of childbirth and family care, necessarily move in and out of the workforce, and help older persons remain productive. They would also provide the leisure time necessary for family life and civic engagement.[7]

Janice retired from the Social Security Administration at the age of fifty-three. Since her formal retirement, she has immersed herself in volunteering and caring for the people around her. She befriended a poor immigrant family, providing compassion and care and helping with the family's needs. She also leads the older adult ministry efforts at the state level for the Church of God in Michigan. She is actively involved in the lives of her children and grandchildren; she even spent nine weeks in Europe, where her daughter's family now lives. She also returned to school and five years ago received a master's degree in religious education. Today, at the age of sixty-seven, Janice is thinking about going back to school again to study gerontology and perhaps become a chaplain who ministers with the elderly. Janice is a great example of an older adult who is weaving work, school, family, and volunteering into her retirement years.

The way boomers are planning out their retirement is as varied as each of them are as individuals. Although the trend to start a new career at fifty-five or sixty is growing, there are still many adults who are approaching retirement with the plan to spend time with family and pursue leisure activities, while others are interested in volunteering significant portions of their time. Regardless of the specific things boomers do during retirement, the overarching theme is that they want to stay active and involved with life, not relegated to a rocking chair on the porch or a recliner in front of the television.

## The Big Three

A number of years ago, I asked some of my aunts and uncles who were in their fifties their thoughts about retirement and specifically what recommendations they had for those who are approaching retirement. Most of them said two things: "Make sure you know how you are going to fill your time" and "Be sure your finances are in order." As I've continued to study and talk with people, I've discovered a third topic pressing on the minds of adults as they think about retiring: "Where are we going to live?"

Despite the changing attitudes surrounding retirement, older adults are still concerned with these three primary issues: money, time, and living arrangements.

## Finances

When people think about retirement, the first thing they think about is their finances. Have I saved enough money? Will I outlive my funds? Do I have enough to live the same lifestyle I do now? On and on the worries spin. As I write this book, the financial aspect of retirement is front and center in the minds of people fifty and over because the economy has experienced a major downturn, the worst crisis since the Great Depression. The nightly news, the newspapers, and even the discussions at the local coffee bar center on what people have lost in their 401(k) plans and the horrible condition of their financial portfolios. Some who had planned to retire soon now feel that they will have to keep working indefinitely to make up the money they have lost. And even before the recession, there was evidence that some boomers had not saved enough money for retirement.

On the flip side, there are older adults entering the retirement years who are still choosing to retire. The sixty-three-year-old nursing home administrator I mentioned earlier told me that his part-time job should enable him to leave his actual retirement money untouched at least until he has recovered some of the losses incurred during the market downturn.

Discussion of the financial aspect of retirement could fill a separate book. But in our quest to get a look inside the minds of aging boomers, there are two primary financial issues that we should examine in this one.

First, the topic of Social Security dominates many discussions today. Most people have concluded that the way Social Security worked in the past won't work for us in the future. Ida Mae Fuller, the recipient of the very first Social Security check in 1940, received a total of $22,888.92 before her death at age one hundred, though she had paid in only $24.75. This was no big deal at the time because there were forty-two workers paying into the system for every one beneficiary. Today, it is anticipated that as the baby boom generation retires, there will eventually be only two workers for every retiree.

To combat this problem, the full retirement age for receiving Social Security benefits has been rising gradually from sixty-five (for retirees in the years 1940–2002) to sixty-seven (as of 2027). And there are discussions that it should be raised to age seventy. Some leaders believe that the boomer generation has the ability to help the situation by continuing to work. Boomers could also hurt the system by retiring and forcing taxes to be raised on younger generations. How this plays out is yet to be seen, but you can be sure that the future of Social Security payments is on the minds of almost everyone who is approaching retirement age.

The second and perhaps even greater concern for the boomer generation is the cost of health care. Even if an individual has a decent retirement income, the unknowns of health care may deplete these resources. Fidelity Investments estimates that a sixty-five-year-old couple can expect to spend $240,000 on health care during their retirement years.[8]

**A Christian Look at Finances in Retirement**  In reviewing the secular literature while writing this chapter, I was reminded again of how much emphasis the world puts on our being comfortable and secure during our retirement years. Many Christians have bought in to this mentality without even realizing that it is not biblical. Let's take a look at some specific Scriptures that teach against a self-focused life.

In terms of finances and indulging ourselves, Jesus is pretty clear with his words in Matthew 6:19–21: "Do not store up for yourselves treasures on earth, where moth and rust destroy, and where thieves break in and steal. But store up for yourselves treasures in heaven, where moth and rust do not destroy, and where thieves do not break in and steal. For where your treasure is, there your heart will be also."

Talk about counterculture! Nearly everything we learn about retirement from an early age is to save, save, save. Is it really possible to change this mind-set?

I talked with a friend in her fifties who has decided along with her husband to stop putting money into a retirement account for the next few years. This has freed up nearly $1,000 a month that they are choosing to give to a building project at their church. Do you think a financial adviser would consider this such a good idea? Especially at their age? But they are finding freedom in it, letting go of this life, which is only temporal, and keeping their eyes on the eternal. It is a tangible, practical way for them to truly trust God for all their needs.

Saving isn't all bad. Proverbs 21:20 reminds us that a man who spends everything is foolish. But saving can become an obsession that leaves little room for God. Jesus explains this well in His parable about the rich fool in Luke 12. In this parable, a rich man produced a good crop and did not have room to store everything, so he tore down his barns and built bigger ones to hold all of his stuff. Verse 19 sounds very familiar to those who take a worldly view of retirement: "And [the rich man] says to himself, 'You have plenty of good things laid up for many years. Take life easy; eat, drink and be merry.'" Saving should not be about accumulating more or being able to live in the lap of luxury. Saving is simply being responsible to set aside enough to provide for our needs.

## Time

While eating pizza with the parents of one of my childhood friends, I brought up the topic of retirement. Darrell retired from a corporate job in 2003 at the age of fifty-six. He currently fills his day as a volunteer for The Gideons International (a ministry committed to personal evangelism and Bible distribution), serves as an elder at his church, travels with his RV and boat, goes to ball games, and visits the grandchildren. In many of these activities he is accompanied by his wife, Kaye, who also does volunteer work in the community. When I asked him how he got involved serving with The Gideons, he related that about a year before his retirement, he began to investigate what he wanted to do in his retirement years. The ministry of The Gideons had always intrigued him, and as he learned more about the organization's work, he decided to give a portion of his time to the effort. He also made a "bucket list" of all the things he wanted to do before he died, and this has become a guide for him in his retirement years.

Interestingly, Darrell has always been a planner—that's what made him good at his job and also why he is finding satisfaction in retirement. Many people, however, spend a lot of time and energy on the financial aspect of retirement but fail to plan how they will fill their days.

Most retirees are able to fill their time in retirement using what is known as the consolidation approach.[9] If we think about our lives, we will recognize that we do a number of things in one day. We go to work, talk with our family, interact with our neighbors, volunteer in the community, go to church, and perhaps indulge in a little recreation. The consolidation approach suggests that when work is removed from the life of an older adult, the person makes up for that loss by filling it with the other things that have been a part of his or her life. For example, a person may take a little longer to linger over the newspaper and the morning cup of coffee, spend more time doing household chores, take an extended time to help a neighbor, and still have time to play eighteen holes of golf with friends and participate in a church Bible study. None of these activities are new; there is just more time to participate in each one of them.

For some people, however, their work has consumed their entire lives, and retirement can leave them feeling restless, bored, and even depressed. Because they did not have strong relationships or interests outside of the work environment, they may have a hard time replacing the lost role of employment. This same thing can happen with women who have spent the majority of their time raising children and have not pursued or developed any interests or hobbies beyond those of their children.

So what do people do in retirement? Typical activities include volunteering in the community or for a church, pursuing lifelong learning, and traveling. Many people use retirement as a chance to develop and enjoy hobbies such as woodworking, dancing, painting, and camping. A number of retirees relish spending time with their grandchildren, even providing child care. And the number of older adults working part time in retirement is expected to increase.

**A Christian Look at What to Do During Retirement** Just as our culture has negatively influenced our view of the financial side of retirement, we also have a mistaken perception of how we are to spend our time in retirement. I've had more than one older adult in a church say something like "I've done my time, Amy. I've paid my dues. It's time for me to relax and let someone else take over" or "I've earned the right to enjoy myself." Nothing could be further from what the Bible teaches, and yet over time, we have begun to accept society's views of retirement and not challenge this attitude among believers.

Nearly every godly character in Scripture who lived into the later years was actively working for God. The apostle John was in his nineties when he wrote the book of Revelation from his place of imprisonment on the island of Patmos, Greece. Moses was eighty years old when he led the Israelites from Egypt across the desert and to the edge of the Promised Land. You will notice in Exodus 4 that Moses came up with a number of excuses why he should not be God's chosen man, but nowhere does he mention his age as one of them.

## Living Arrangements

One question for people to consider when planning their retirement years is where they are going to live. Should they downsize their home or stay in their current location? Do they move closer to grandchildren, or do they move somewhere with an attractive retirement lifestyle? Del Webb, the nation's leader in building communities for active older adults, found in a recent survey that 59 percent of baby boomers plan to relocate upon retirement.[10] This is quite different from the previous generation, who for the most part stayed in the same community their entire lives. Because boomers have been more mobile throughout their careers, it is not as difficult for them to pick up and move during retirement. Boomers often lack the sentimental attachment to the family home felt in previous generations.

What are the boomers' options?

- *Staying in their current location.* Despite the trend to move, many older adults will choose to stay in their current home and retire in the community where they have been living most recently. This is where they have established friendships and community connections. People who stay put may have more social support as they age and their care needs increase. Retirees may stay in the same community but downsize to a smaller home. This helps with finances and can also allow adults to simplify their lives and get a fresh start in retirement.

- *Moving to a college town.* It is increasingly popular for older adults to move to a college community where they can enjoy many of the cultural, educational, and athletic opportunities that abound in these areas. Some college communities are building retirement communities within walking distance of the campus so that retirees can easily take part in the life of the college.

- *Relocating to a fifty-five-plus active adult community.* These living environments, designed for active retirees, offer resort-style living, with fitness centers, swimming pools, golf courses, and other recreational opportunities. We typically think of these communities being in locations such as Florida or Arizona, but they have sprung up in most large metropolitan areas and some smaller cities. Even some leading-edge boomers who have not retired are choosing to live in these communities.

- *Moving where children and grandchildren live.* As noted in Chapter Four, boomers intend to spend large amounts of time with family, and for some this means relocating to where their children live.

- *Maintaining two homes.* Some retirees choose to live part of the year in a northern climate and the other half of the year somewhere warmer.

**A Christian Look at Where to Live in Retirement** Genesis 12 records the story of Abram, who in his old age (perhaps what we would consider his retirement years) uprooted his family and moved to a new home simply because God told him to. Not everyone receives such crystal-clear directions about where to live, but the point is that in all decisions, we need to be seeking what God wants—even in regard to our living arrangements.

Earl and Pat Ferguson had no intention of moving into Carillon, a fifty-five-plus community, until God impressed on them the ministry He could do through them if they lived there. Earl had just finished a thirty-eight-year ministry as a senior pastor when he was asked to become a leader in one of Community Christian Church's multisite campuses at Carillon. Since the Fergusons took on the leadership role of the church, the Sunday morning service attendance has grown from 50 to 150.

The church hosts small group Bible studies, a grief support group, and other activities that reach out to the nearly 3,600 adults who live in Carillon. Earl and Pat have seen a number of older adults come to Christ and begin serving Him. And the church is now being asked to help other retirement communities that want to start churches.[11]

The Fergusons' willingness to move has put them in a prime place for significant ministry. Older adults may be led to downsize their home and work on the mission field, while some may be called to move closer to their children who need support. Others make the choice to stay in their own home and serve in the community where they have built long-term relationships. Regardless of where people live during their retirement years, older adults need to be challenged to look beyond their own selfish desires in terms of housing and instead see the places where God wants them to serve.

## Retirement in the Bible?

Until recently, I would passionately tell anyone who would listen that retirement is never mentioned in the Bible. But one day in Bible study, I came across a passage that does speak of retiring: "Men twenty-five years old or more shall come to take part in the work at the Tent of Meeting, but at the age of fifty, they must retire from their regular service and work no longer. They may assist their brothers in performing their duties at the Tent of Meeting, but they themselves must not do the work" (Numbers 8:24–26). The English Standard Version says it this way: "They shall withdraw from the duty of the service and serve no more."

This portion of Scripture is part of some lengthy instructions given to Moses regarding the tabernacle in the wilderness. According to God's direction, the Levites were to be set apart from the other Israelite tribes as the ones who served at the Tent of Meeting (the tabernacle). In their early years, the work involved carrying the tabernacle and the utensils used in the tabernacle. This required physical strength and hard labor. After age fifty, God relieved them of these strenuous physical duties, but they were not given a gold watch and encouraged to relax and take it easy. Verse 26 says they were to "assist their brothers" and, in the King James Version, to "keep the charge," meaning they were to watch and guard the structure and ordinances regarding God's dwelling place.

There was a natural acceptance that the physical body does decline and may not be able to handle demanding physical tasks. But these ordained servants of God were still to be mentors to the younger priests and were to help out in whatever way they could. They retired from the job of their younger days and entered into a new job of service to God in the later years of their lives.

The crystal-clear message in the Bible is that we never retire from our walk with God or our service to Him. Though the form of this service may change depending on the season of our lives, Scripture commands us to continue growing in Christ and serving Him until He chooses to take us home.

## The Church and Retirement

Until now, the Christian community has not been very strategic or intentional in ministering to people who are approaching or have entered the retirement phase of life. Perhaps we've been too accepting of the way retirement has been viewed in the past or we just haven't had enough retired people in our congregations to really focus on this. There are a number of things the church can do to begin to reshape the world's view of retirement and help individuals navigate this season of life.

One of the most obvious but most difficult things is to *teach against the culture*. Romans 12:2 reminds us that we should not conform to the pattern of this world. However, if we were to be honest, retirement is one area where many Christians are conforming to the world's view. It is so subtle that people don't even realize how they have bought in to the mentality of focusing on entertainment and leisure pursuits in the second half of life. Even young people need to be taught from the pulpit, in Sunday school classes, through small groups, and in any other venue that to be a true follower of Christ, "you should look not only to your own interests, but also to the interests of others" (Philippians 2:4).

A second way the church can minister is by *helping people discover ways to use their hobbies and interests as ministry*. This requires people to recognize that church is more than where they go on Sunday; it is something they live out every moment of their lives. For example, there is nothing inherently wrong with golfing a few days every week, but how much better for the Kingdom would it be if those golf outings were regarded as divine appointments to interact with, love, and serve non-Christians? This recalls to mind the man mentioned earlier who used his car wash business to interact with members of younger generations and bring them to Christ.

RV groups are popular among some segments of retirees. These clubs often travel to a campsite for a few days every month. But some more purposeful groups have turned their love of traveling into opportunities for mission work. Christian schools, homeless missions, camps, and a host of other agencies use these retirees to do maintenance work, construction projects, and a variety of other jobs. A quick Internet search will reveal a number of formal ministries that welcome the help of RV travelers.

People need to be challenged to use their interests to do Kingdom work. All it may take is exposure to an opportunity that will allow them to use what they enjoy doing to make a mark for eternity.

Another important way for church leaders to help people in this particular season is to *recognize that retirement is a major life transition*. Retirement is not a onetime event, but it is often depicted that way. Have the farewell dinner, receive the gold watch, take home your box of personal belongings from the office, and presto! you're retired? It just doesn't work like that. Like getting married or having a baby, the big event occurs at a specific time, but the reality of living in the aftermath is a day-by-day process filling a whole season of life.

Robert Atchley, a scholar in the field of aging, studied retirement extensively and identified a number of phases of retirement
that people may go through.[12] He presented these phases years
ago, but they still provide a great framework for us as we think
about the various places to enter into people's lives and minister
to them.

Phase 1 is called preretirement. It's when a person sets the
date for retirement and begins to envision what life will be like
when he or she no longer goes to work every day. This is a key
time for the church to step in. Churches have premarital counseling and classes on preparing for the adolescent years of parenting—why not offer classes or a counseling session on preparing
for retirement, from a biblical perspective? When asked about
formal retirement preparation, most adults will say they met with
a financial planner or attended a financial planning workshop
sponsored by their employer, but very few adults have attended
a comprehensive retirement seminar that asks them to consider
how they will spend their time in retirement and how retirement
will affect their relationships, specifically their marriage and their
friendships. This is the kind of soul-searching that might be done
in a retreat setting or over a long conversation with a few
Christian mentors. It should involve prayer and seeking the
Lord, asking Him what He has for this new phase of life.

The second phase is what people do immediately after they
retire. Atchley suggests that people often take one of three paths.
Some jump right into a honeymoon phase. They act like they
are on an indefinite vacation, trying to do everything they wanted
to do while they were working but didn't have the time to do.
Often this includes lots of travel and pursuing hobbies. This is
not an easy stage to jump into with effective ministry. People do
not feel they have any need for help because to them everything
is going great!

Some may not take the honeymoon path and instead fall
into an immediate retirement routine. These individuals had a
realistic view of retirement and more than likely planned how

they would spend their time during their preretirement phase. Often when these people were working, they had full and active lives outside their jobs, and so it is easy for them to adapt to a retirement schedule, perhaps with volunteer activities, part-time work, or other interests.

A third path for some people is the rest-and-relaxation stage. People who have had busy and demanding careers often choose to do very little in their early retirement years. They want to do nothing more than relax. When I was first serving in older adult ministry (and didn't yet understand these phases), I approached a Christian man who had recently retired from his job as a high school chemistry teacher. I asked him if he would work alongside me in developing an educational ministry for older adults in the community. He was quick to say that he didn't want to do anything for a while except sit in a chair and read. He needed time to rest. Interestingly, after some time of doing nothing, he became one of my best and most active volunteers.

Although these three paths do not provide lots of open doors for the church to intervene, there are ways for the church to communicate the desire to walk with people as they navigate these early stages of retirement.

First Evangelical Free Church in Fullerton, California, attempts to do this by talking one-on-one with people who are approaching retirement or have just retired. The senior adult pastor gives them his blessing to take six months to relax, travel, and do whatever they want. In other words, he tells them it is OK to enjoy the honeymoon or relaxation phase of retirement. After the six months have passed, he again meets with the retirees to talk about their priorities and the many opportunities for service that exist for them in their retirement years.

After a period of honeymooning or relaxing, a few people may experience a phase of disenchantment, a time of uncertainty or even disappointment about retirement. The way they envisioned this season during the preretirement phase turns out not to have been realistic. A permanent state of resting is not fulfilling, nor can one sustain a constant state of vacationing. When things slow down or change, they find themselves having to reinvent a life suitable for retirement. Another reason for disenchantment arises when the situation one expects in retirement is disrupted. This most often happens when a spouse becomes ill or dies or when the retiree's own health declines.

This phase is a crisis period for the retiree and, if navigated correctly, can be a great time for spiritual growth for both the Christian and the non-Christian. Too often retirees are expected to view retirement as a wonderful time of life with no worries or challenges, but this is not realistic. Moving from work to retirement is a major life transition, and it is not unusual for people to experience feelings of grief. People may suffer with loneliness due to a loss of regular contact with coworkers. Some may be faced with the stress of caring for a spouse who is ill while others struggle to accept that the leisure activities they planned for retirement are not satisfying. Churches can encourage adults who are in the disenchantment phase to intentionally spend time with God and grow closer to Him while seeking out His purpose for their lives. Mentioning some of the difficulties of retirement in a sermon and offering to pray for those who are struggling can help people know they are not alone. The care, compassion, and counseling that a church offers may be very helpful to a retiree in the disenchantment phase.

Phase four is reorientation, and this is a crucial place for the church to intervene with ministry and biblical teaching. Reorientation occurs after the honeymoon period, rest period, or disenchantment phase and is a time when people take stock of their lives and reorder their priorities.

Of all the phases, this may be the one where the church can have the most influence. Offering small group Bible studies where people can discuss their fears and dreams regarding this season of life can be very beneficial. While a conference might be a great way to get people thinking about life issues, opportunities for discussion seem to be the most desired. A professor who received a grant from the U.S. Administration on Aging created eight television programs on preretirement education. Then he and several colleagues developed a series of seminars at which one of these programs was viewed and discussion followed. More than nine hundred people participated. Interestingly, what the participants appreciated most was not the actual information gleaned so much as the opportunity to discuss their fears and concerns about retirement with other people in their peer group.[13]

Phase five begins when people comfortably enter into a retirement routine. Some may be able to do this quickly after leaving employment; others need more time.

The last phase defined by Atchley is the termination of retirement. This occurs when people experience illness and disability and become more dependent on others.

It is important to note that not everyone goes through all of these phases, nor is there a particular time when each stage occurs. However, recognizing the different stages people are experiencing and intervening with meaningful ministry can be an effective way of leading people into a God-focused retirement plan.

A final way the church can help people is by *shining a light on individuals who are living out a God-honoring retirement*. We all need mentors for all the different stages of our lives, and there is a need for those who have retired successfully to be mentoring the soon-to-be-retired.

The way Bob and Deannie are living out their lives in retirement provides an example for many in their church and community to follow. In fact, when I visited this couple, they told me that certain adults in their church who are ten years younger than they are have said, "We want to pattern our retirement years after you."

Bob was a corporate executive who was downsized at age fifty-four. He and Deannie spent the first year and a half of retirement completely focused on renovating a new home, but during this time, one of the pastors at his church was praying for him.

Through the pastor's persistence and a small group Bible study on Henry Blackaby's *Experiencing God*, Bob began leading the Career Center ministry through his church. He was considered a part of the church staff, though unpaid, and spent about six hours a day four days a week managing the Career Center. This ministry was open to anyone in the community looking for employment, and the center provided a place for them to work on their résumés, use the telephone, and take inventories to determine their personal skill sets.

Bob used his business experience and his skills in recruiting and sales to form relationships with many of the leading companies in the city. These companies would come to the church on certain days to conduct interviews with interested individuals. They helped some twenty to thirty people every week.

Deannie's retirement experience has been similar, though she said she has been learning that she doesn't always have to be busy, that she can instead wait for the Lord to show her opportunities to speak of God to those who cross her path. She told me, "I'm more prayerful now to watch for where God is at work around me, rather than just filling up my calendar. My goal is to slow down and ask God what He wants me to do."

The couple have participated in a number of overseas mission trips with their church, and the two of them also led the volunteer ministry at their church for more than three years. This was again an unpaid staff position where they were expected to participate in church staff meetings and to enjoy both the privileges and responsibilities that come with being on a church staff.

The retirement season of life ebbs and flows just like other seasons, and this has happened in Bob and Deannie's lives. A few years ago, Deannie was diagnosed with cancer, so Bob began to step out of some of his ministry roles in order to care for his wife. As her condition improved and she needed less daily care, Bob prayed, asking what God wanted him to do next.

He said, "My idea of retirement was different from God's." Bob thought he would spend his time golfing and taking it easy after a pressure-filled career. Thank goodness Bob and Deannie were sensitive to God's calling on their lives. And thank goodness a pastor believed God had more for this couple than a static, leisure-filled retirement. May God put into all of our hearts a burning desire to call people out of the world's retirement and into God's purposeful retirement.

# Part Three

## HARNESSING THE POTENTIAL: IMPLICATIONS FOR THE CHURCH

# 6

# LETTING GO OF THE "ONE SIZE FITS ALL" MENTALITY

May I ask you to do a little exercise for me? Without thinking too hard about it, what comes to your mind when you think of senior adult ministry? Perhaps your ideas have started to change after reading the first half of this book. If that's the case, try to reflect on what you thought of senior adult ministry before picking up this resource. Be honest. Potlucks? Bus trips? A patriotic themed dinner and program? A barbershop quartet?

There is nothing inherently wrong with any of these activities, but the truth is that these programs, which have been somewhat effective at reaching senior adults for the past thirty years, are not going to reach the new generation of older adults.

A few months ago, I was talking with a leader who provides oversight to older adult ministries at the denominational level. We were discussing how to reach the younger set of fifty-and-over adults and how things would have to change. She said, "I believed for quite some time that if we would just wait long enough—wait for the boomers to get further along in their aging process—they would naturally fold into the existing senior adult ministry. But now I know that was faulty thinking." Her comment brought to my mind an older man who once said, "I can't wait until these younger folks get old so we can start singing the hymns again at church!" It still makes me chuckle.

Ministry with this generation will look different now *and* in the future. It will never resemble the senior adult ministry of the past because this new generation of older adults is completely different from previous generations.

The health care industry recognizes that twenty or thirty years from now, when the boomers need more medical care, nursing homes will have to look different. Already they are preparing by creating a more customer-focused approach to care in which adults have more choices regarding meals and activities. Nursing homes in the future will have more private rooms and wireless Internet access. The interest in people staying in their own homes as they age has created a growing market for bringing services into people's homes rather than expecting adults to move to nursing homes. All of these changes are attempts to prepare for the needs of the new old.

Changes like these are inevitable as we move through the course of life and ministry. And older adult ministry is no exception. To effectively reach out and minister with the new generation of the fifty-and-over, older adult ministry will have to change in significant ways.

## Older Adults: Not All Alike

It is not uncommon for me to receive an e-mail or a phone call from a church leader who says, "We'd like to set up a seniors program. Can you help us?" I usually begin by encouraging the leader to let go of the idea that one single program is the answer. Frankly, everything we've been discussing so far in this book leads to the conclusion that there cannot be one stand-alone program to reach the many older adults in our communities.

A common myth regarding aging is that older people are all alike. It's as if someone reaches sixty or seventy or whatever arbitrary number and then automatically drives slower, goes to bed earlier, and becomes forgetful. Research as well as day-to-day interaction with a variety of older adults will quickly disprove this myth. Some drive very fast, stay up way past midnight, and have minds that are sharp as a tack! So the reality is we become more diverse as we age.

If you gather a roomful of preschoolers, you will find that developmentally, they are basically doing the same things. Some may be slightly ahead of others, but they are all mastering such skills as identifying colors and shapes, throwing a ball, and learning how to interact socially with teachers and other kids.

But as we get older, our differences increase. By the age of eighty, some people have never left the state in which they were born while others have traveled all over the world. Some have doctorate degrees, and others never finished high school. There are some who have experienced a divorce and some who never married. Some may be working while others have been retired for two decades.

One of the greatest differences among people is the status of their health and their physical capabilities. There are many older adults who are quite active and in great shape physically, while others are frail and living with disabilities.

The bottom line is that we all have unique life experiences that shape us into the people we are. This kind of diversity among people requires diverse ministries.

## Expanding the Ministry

One way to ensure that our ministries reflect the diversity of older adults is to create ministries that respond to the different methods of defining age.

Chronological age is based on what the birth certificate says. The U.S. Department of Labor defines an "older worker" as anyone over the age of forty.[1] McDonald's gives you the seniors' discount on a cup of coffee at the age of fifty-five. Both of these go by chronological age. They don't care if a person is fifty and in a wheelchair or eighty-five and making millions of dollars a year.

There is value to having some ministries designed to reach a specific age group of people. Connecting with others in the same generation can be rewarding as people share common experiences and memories.

Richard and Leona Bergstrom lead the Second Half Ministries at Northshore Baptist Church in Bothell, Washington. A few years ago, they formed a focus group of adults in the fifty-to-seventy age range and discovered that for many of these people, the opportunity to have fun with their peers was very appealing. From this came the idea for the "Baby Boomer Bash," a party featuring Beatles music, decorations in orange and yellow, pizza, and dancing. It was an opportunity to celebrate and affirm people who were in this specific life stage.

A second way of defining age is functional age. This has more to do with the health and physical capabilities of an individual rather than numerical age. A hiking trip or even an activity that requires driving after dark is more likely to appeal to those whose functional age supports them participating in these activities. The older adult ministry at Peninsula Covenant Church in Redwood City, California, hosted a tour to Israel and invited all ages to participate. The majority of the people were in their forties, fifties, and sixties, but there were adults in their eighties too—because their functional age made it possible for them to participate fully in the tour.

Psychological age is the third definition of aging and refers to how old someone feels. Some may think it strange for a couple in their seventies to attend a contemporary worship concert, but they may actually enjoy this particular style of music. We never want to limit older adults or put them in a box by not including them in certain events or activities. Paul Stetler, minister with adults fifty and better at LifeBridge Christian Church in Longmont, Colorado, told me about a camping trip primarily intended for those in the fifty-to-sixty age range. While the majority of couples who participated were this age, one couple in their eighties joined the group and everyone enjoyed having them along. Psychologically, they did not feel old, and they wanted to take part in the trip.

A fourth way of defining age is known as social age: allowing the stage of life we are in dictate how old we are. For example, a study conducted by the Pew Research Group found that 23 percent of people believe old age begins at retirement and 15 percent believe it begins when you have grandchildren. Both of these are examples of social age, for some people retire at fifty while others work until their eighties. Interestingly, the study also indicated that 79 percent of respondents believe old age begins at eighty-five (this would be an example of defining age chronologically) and 76 percent said old age begins when someone can't live independently (an example of functional age).[2]

Hosting a grandparenting conference or leading a four-week Bible study on preparing for retirement are ministries that respond to social age. It doesn't matter if someone is becoming a grandparent for the first time at forty or at seventy; the conference is intended to reach those who are in the grandparenting role.

The bottom line is that we can't fool ourselves into thinking a potluck luncheon will appeal to everybody who is older, and the reality is, it probably never did. A "one size fits all" approach to ministry is typically not effective with any age group, but it is most certainly not going to work with those in the over-fifty set.

## Integrating Older Adults into the Entire Church

When I was growing up, my home church held an annual "promotion Sunday." As children, we looked forward to this special event, marking the completion of one Sunday school grade and the move up to the next. We were proud of our accomplishment and excited to meet our new teacher. But as adults, we typically do not like situations like this. We don't want to be "promoted" and told that we must fit into a certain mold. Most of us would like to be known for who we are as unique individuals, not categorized by our age.

In the academic literature, this is called *age-grading*, and it refers to using age to dictate what opportunities and privileges people can enjoy. Society has adopted expectations as to when people should get married, have their first child, and retire from work. We are pressured to fit into certain categories. Rather than making choices based on who we are in Christ, we let others dictate the roles we play.

Age-grading pops up where we don't expect it. I've asked young people to tell me their reactions to a thirty-year-old planning a career change and then to a sixty-five-year-old contemplating the same sort of move. The young adults find nothing unusual about the thirty-year-old's plan but often react strongly to the older man's plan, making comments like "Why would someone want a new job when he should be getting ready to retire?" Age-grading has us assume that someone who is sixty-five should be retiring, not ramping up for a new career.

And this thinking does not just affect young people. We have all been conditioned to view some experiences as normal behavior for a person's age and other activities as abnormal. For example, we may think it is quite appropriate for our twenty-five-year-old niece to be getting married, but we have reservations about our eighty-five-year-old father getting married—especially if he is marrying a thirty-year-old woman!!

About a year ago, while visiting a church, I met a former state senator who was in his seventies. I asked if he participated in his church's weekly senior adult program. He looked at me like I was crazy and said, "I don't want to be with those old people!" He proceeded to tell me about his intergenerational Sunday school class, which included young families, singles, and retirees. He resisted the label of being old and found more in common with a group of people of varying ages. He had found his place to belong at the church and his place to serve, but for him, it was not within the formal older adult program.

We may use age-grading within the church without even realizing it. We think the older adults won't like contemporary music, so we don't include them in discussions regarding music changes or ask them to be involved with the planning and execution of worship services. We assume that older adults have no desire to serve overseas on a mission trip or teach a group of junior high boys, so we never invite them to participate.

The key is to not view older adults as a separate group but instead as an integral part of the church as a whole. I've found that the best and most practical way to implement this is by involving older adults in every aspect of the church's ministry.

Attending women's ministry events, singing on the worship team, serving the homeless, teaching in the children's ministry and every ministry in between—all should be open and available to older adults.

However, some churches measure the success of their ministries by how many people of a certain age group or category are attending a particular Bible study or activity. For example, in a small group–driven church, the older adult ministry director may be evaluated on the basis of how many small groups there are for people over fifty. This mentality does more harm than good. Take, for instance, the case of a sixty-two-year-old woman who has a passion for mentoring young moms. She immerses herself in the women's ministry and spends hours every week meeting one-on-one with young women, encouraging and discipling them. Her own relationship with God is growing as she pours out her heart in prayer regarding the women she is serving. The older adult minister meets with her regularly offering her tools and resources on mentoring, which he thoroughly enjoys and so does she.

And yet he always feels pressured to convince this vibrant woman to lead a small group Bible study for adults who are fifty-plus, which would take time away from her mentoring ministry.

The pressure this pastor experiences comes from the way this church measures success—in this case, the number of small groups for people age fifty and over. Even though this particular minister appears to be doing a fantastic job leading this woman into significant, Kingdom-minded ministry, he is treated as a failure at his "real" job—getting fifty-and-over adults into small groups.

A far-fetched example? Unfortunately, it is not. Too often those of us who work and lead in churches tend to be territorial with respect to our ministries. Sometimes it is as if we are saying, "Keep your hands off *my* volunteer" or "She belongs in *my* ministry." Not only is this a poor way to accomplish God's work through the local church, but it will also turn away older adults who do not want to be labeled or told they must fit into a certain slot.

Programs, classes, and groups that are specifically designed for the needs of the older population are valuable and have a place, but the success of a ministry can never be measured solely by how many older adults come to these events. Our goal should be to involve older adults in every aspect of the church, encouraging them to grow in their relationship with God and unleashing them to serve Him wholeheartedly.

One way to measure the success of an older adult ministry is by counting how many older adults are involved in a serving role either inside or outside the church. I once sent an e-mail to our entire church staff, asking them to send me the names of the adults who were over the age of fifty-five serving in some capacity in their particular area of ministry. The replies included men serving on the elder board, an older adult playing the trumpet in the worship band, a sixty-year-old man overseeing the transportation ministry, retired men and women visiting the sick, and many other individuals doing many other jobs. Writing down these names helped all of us realize that nearly every ministry in the church, from the children's ministry to the worship department, relied to some extent on older adults.

A second way to measure success is to pay specific attention to the adults over fifty who are not participating in any area of ministry. Most churches have a number of boomer and older adults who are actively involved in the life of the church, and many of their needs are being met through other ministries. Rather than spending all of our energy trying to convince these people to come to a fifty-plus ministry event, we should focus our efforts on the older adults who are unconnected. The hope is that the connected will find some value in our events, but our success should be measured by how many folks attend who have never been involved beyond the Sunday worship service.

## Avoiding Certain Words

The expression "senior citizens" originated in the 1930s as a euphemism to refer to people who were elderly or aged. In recent years, the expression has often been reduced to a single word, *seniors*. For the most part, when churches adopted the word *senior* to identify a new ministry area (senior adult ministry), people accepted it. However, among the new generation of older adults, this term is often not viewed in a positive light.

Today, most people over the age of fifty perceive a senior as someone they are not. *Old, elderly, senior,* and *golden-ager* are all words that have negative connotations attached to them.

Like it or not, to appeal to aging baby boomers, new terms are needed. This is a challenge for many churches and organizations. To reach a specific group of people, we need a way of defining them, yet one of the primary lessons we are learning is that today's older adults do not like to be labeled and do not like anything that smacks of old age. One pastor told me that it is a huge dilemma to choose a name and develop an identity that won't repel people.

Some churches find success by using positive terms for their ministries, such as "Adults Fifty and Better," "Life After Fifty," or "Second Half Ministries." A number of churches and national ministries are using the term *encore* or *encore generation* to describe this new group of older adults. When a concert or performance ends and we stand to cheer and applaud, we are pleading for an encore. Often the performer has saved the best for last, and the audience is saying, "Please come back out and give us some more." Similarly, older adults have an opportunity to come back on stage and give more of their time and talents to further God's Kingdom.

Other churches are completely eliminating the age connotations associated with their ministry. The older adult ministry at Peninsula Covenant Church in Redwood City, California, uses the name "Plus." Rod Toews, the pastor of Plus Ministries, explains that the ministry is trying to focus on people in a certain life stage rather than on people of a certain numerical age. And the name Plus defines one of the ministry's goals: to add something to people's lives.

Green Acres Baptist Church in Tyler, Texas, has a ministry called Adult Impact. The ministry seeks to engage any adult in meaningful service, but there is an intentional focus on reaching the baby boomer. Kevin Burdette, the minister of Adult Impact, took on the challenge of creating a ministry with aging baby boomers when it was obvious that the existing older adult ministry (called Forerunners) was not going to reach them. As Kevin and his team searched to give the ministry an identity, they found that any title that suggested age was not well received. There are intentional events and ministries that are designed to support and engage the aging baby boomer, but Kevin is careful about using age as a label.

There is no one term that all older adults are happy to use in describing themselves. There may never be one single term. You will have to experiment in your unique ministry context to find the best way to communicate and reach people in this evolving stage of life.

A second consideration regarding our terminology may seem petty, but it communicates much about the vision and focus of the ministry. It is as simple as considering if our ministry is *to* older adults or *with* and *through* older adults. A ministry *to* older adults implies that we are doing something for them—catering to their needs, their wants, their desires. A ministry *with* and *through* older adults suggests that the ministry is something we do together, a place where older adults are serving one another as well as the church and the community.

Over time, eliminating a few words from our vocabulary and replacing them with new words can have positive results. Existing ministry participants become eager to invite peers to church activities, members of older adult small groups are not embarrassed at being identified as part of "that" age group, and the never involved may now be willing to attend various events. If we really want to change the negative view of aging and realize the benefits in our churches and in our society, we must be willing to change the language we use.

## A Balanced Approach

I was sitting at my parents' kitchen table talking with my eighty-year-old aunt. She was graciously trying to understand the purpose of this book. I explained that while this resource would help churches in ministering with people her age, it was even more focused on ministry with baby boomers, people an entire generation younger than herself. I said with a smile, "They look at things a little differently than your generation." And it was as if a light bulb had gone on in her head. She became more animated and said, "Yeah, they sure *are* different, and I don't understand what it is they *do!* They don't join groups like the Masons or the Kiwanis. What *do* they do?" She is an involved senior adult who participates in activities at the local senior center and enjoys square dancing and sewing. She fits many of the characteristics of her generation in that she is civic-minded and socially involved with her small community. And she recognizes that there are few boomers who participate in the same activities she does, though she doesn't understand why.

As a whole, members of her generation, the builder generation, were (and still are) very loyal to their church, their community, and their family. They attended family gatherings, served on committees, and took part in town meetings without giving much thought as to whether this was something that they wanted to do. They participated simply because "that's what you're supposed to do."

Senior adult ministry naturally took on a similar feel. Thirty or more years ago, a typical ministry with older adults had a highly programmed approach. For example, the local church's program for seniors often included a monthly themed luncheon and a business meeting. The group may have had a president, vice president, secretary, and treasurer. Birthday cards were signed for various group members, a devotional was read, and an offering was usually gathered to support a mission effort or community ministry. Musical entertainment or a guest speaker rounded out the afternoon's activities. Other senior groups met at local restaurants or spent an afternoon playing cards and dominoes. Senior adult ministries were also known for planning travel opportunities and organizing day trips to places of local interest such as botanical gardens, museums, and parks.

Obviously, I've only scratched the surface regarding the various activities some churches have planned for their seniors. But as I reflect back to my early days of leading older adult ministry, I know that I oversaw many of the same types of activities that I've just mentioned. Mind you, these activities are not wrong in and of themselves. Every ministry and every generation of people need opportunities for connection. The social or fellowship aspect of ministry is an important component in helping people put down roots that will give them the confidence to continue growing in Christ and serving Him. But there are a few crucial things we must embrace if we are going to have future older adult ministries that have a maximum impact on people's lives and ultimately fruitful results for God's Kingdom.

First, members of the boomer generation and people just slightly older are not going to respond to the same type of ministry as the generation before them. For one thing, they may enjoy some of the same activities (such as going out to dinner or attending a concert), but if they are asked to participate with the current older group, they often decline, saying, "I'm not that old." Everything we've talked about to this point in the book has led us to know that most aging boomers shy away from anything that resembles being old. Even if an activity isn't exclusively for members of the builder generation, if they perceive it as such, they won't come.

One church leader told me about an event his church was hosting with the hope of appealing to boomers. As he was inviting and encouraging people to attend, one man said something like "If I see one of those walkers or canes in the parking lot, I'm turning around and going home!" Although this is a rather selfish and shortsighted comment, it does illustrate just how strongly some boomers feel about being asked to participate in an activity they think is for older people. We should think twice about asking leading-edge boomers to participate in the same activity or group with other adults who are the age of their parents. Many boomers are willing to help with events for the older set, but they don't want to socialize with them.

Boomers also tend to be far less driven by programs than the builder generation. They like activities that seem purposeful to them, that promote health and wellness and keep them feeling young. They are less interested in attending a meeting "just because they're supposed to" and more interested in involving themselves in something they consider productive and worthwhile. For example, a ministry targeted toward the boomer generation might best resemble a day of serving together at a local homeless shelter followed by dinner together and a time of reflection.

Another key reason we must take a fresh look at how we minister with older adults is that the fellowship component of older adult ministries has often been overemphasized while other important aspects have been neglected. Go back and consider the list you compiled at the beginning of this chapter. How many of the activities you identified were social? Our initial thoughts about senior adult ministry usually do not bring up ideas of older people working on a Habitat for Humanity house or serving in a foreign country.

Many senior adult ministries have done a great job providing fellowship for older members of a congregation that are feeling displaced and marginalized. However, most of these ministries are sorely out of balance, lacking an emphasis on spiritual growth, evangelism, and service.

Unfortunately, some church leaders have perpetuated this lack of balance because of their incorrect perception of what an older adult ministry is. I'm sure you are familiar with churches that have changed the style of their worship services and changed church programs in order to reach young families and the unchurched. This can have great results with new people coming to Christ and growing in Him. However, church leaders make a major mistake in how they go about ministering with the older generation in the midst of these changes. Some churches will attempt to deal with disgruntled older adults by designating or hiring a leader exclusively for the senior adult ministry. The purpose of this ministry (in their eyes) is to "keep the older people happy so they won't complain and cause problems regarding the changes in the church."

This mentality immediately compartmentalizes older adults and sees them as not central to the mission of the church. If their wisdom, talents, time, and skills are not necessary for the health and growth of the church, then why not just be a group that gets together to have fun? I'm convinced this is one reason we've seen an overemphasis on social activities among many older adult ministries.

A second reason the fellowship emphasis has taken center stage can be traced to what we identified in the chapter on retirement. Our culture has led us to believe that the later years of life should be a time to focus on ourselves—to enjoy our years of hard labor by relaxing and even letting others serve us.

Not long ago, I was meeting with some church leaders who wanted to begin an older adult ministry in their local church. When the congregation heard they were planning to hire a pastor to concentrate in this area of ministry, one of the older ladies said, "Finally, we are going to get some attention and someone to focus on us!" This mentality fuels the idea that older adult ministries should be about providing fun activities for older church members, rather than older adults being encouraged to serve others.

In my interaction with a variety of older adult ministries, I find that most leaders want to include evangelism, discipleship, and service in their ministries, but few have intentional and strategic ways of making this happen. As we consider ministry with aging boomers, we must build ministries that include a balance of all of these components.

## The Changing Role of the Older Adult Leader

When you start making significant changes in the overall design and purpose of a ministry, the type of person best suited to be the leader will be different from the one who has led older adult ministry in the past. Regardless of whether the person is a lay leader or a paid church staff member, a minister with aging boomers should have certain characteristics. But first let's take a look at what a minister with boomers is not.

### What a Minister with Aging Boomers Is Not

There are a couple of ways to describe the role many senior adult ministers have assumed over the years.

One model for a senior adult minister has been the role of a chaplain or pastoral care minister. This individual spends a large amount of time caring for the physical, emotional, and spiritual needs of those who are sick and dependent. They are heavily involved with people who are dying and others who are grieving the loss of a spouse or loved one. I'm familiar with a number of churches whose senior adult pastor visits older adults who are homebound or in nursing homes or hospitals nearly every day of the week. In other churches, this ministry leader drives the seniors to doctor's appointments, to the grocery store, or to the barbershop or salon. They may also host Bible studies and activities for the seniors and again work at providing transportation so each of them can participate. For many pastors, their actual title is "pastoral care/senior adult minister."

This ministry is valuable and needed! Too often adults who can no longer transport themselves to church are forgotten. First Baptist Church in Huntsville, Alabama, has a unique ministry for the homebound: the church offers a Sunday school class every Sunday morning that is conducted over the phone. The teacher leads the class from an office at the church, and participants call in on a conference call at a certain prearranged time. Class members listen to the teacher lead the Bible lesson, and they are encouraged to participate in discussion and share prayer requests over the phone.

Ministries that provide care and counsel to the frail members of our society are going to become increasingly important, and those in the boomer generation can be some of the best servants to this segment of people. But—and this is a big but—a pastoral care style of older adult ministry will *not* be an effective way of reaching and unleashing the new generation of older adults. One of the myths of aging is that old age means you are sick and dependent. With advancing years, there is an increased risk of health problems, and in the very late stages of life, dependency can happen. However, most older adults are not yet in this stage, and so a ministry designed to reach the new old must focus on engaging people into meaningful growth and service. A minister responsible for overseeing pastoral care and aging boomers will probably not reach many boomers because the boomers will want to keep their distance from something that sounds "old."

A second model used by senior adult ministers has been that of travel agent, event planner, or tour director. I liken this to the role of cruise director on a large cruise ship. Ministers using this model are constantly planning activities, Bible studies, card groups, and fun outings. The work of planning is time-intensive and takes away from strategically involving others in service opportunities, encouraging people in peer evangelism, and shepherding individuals as they grow in their faith.

## Characteristics of a Minister with Aging Boomers

The job description of a paid minister or lay leader with the new old will depend on the style and organization of his or her church. However, there are a few common characteristics among older adult ministers that help ensure the success of the ministry.

First, the leader must have an unquenchable passion for the people and type of ministry I've been describing in this book. It can't just be a passion for caring for the sick or planning activities for older people. It has to be a passion to see adults in the fifty-plus age group fully engaged in using their gifts, experiences, and talents for the sake of Christ. It needs to be a passion that longs to see boomers finding their way to God and growing deeper in their daily and personal worship of Him. It has to be a passion that will cause the leader to work tenaciously at discipling these adults to lay down a self-centered, me-focused lifestyle and instead take incredible risks for God.

Passion will enhance the ministry because it keeps the leader focused during difficult times. For more than fifteen years, I've been talking, praying, leading, writing, teaching, and speaking to anyone who will listen about the importance of older adult ministry and its implications for the church and the world. I don't even want to count the times my challenges have fallen on deaf ears. If I weren't completely passionate about this ministry, I'm sure I would have quit by now.

The leader must be passionate about his or her ministry in order to be a model to the older adults he or she serves. If the goals are for aging adults to have a vibrant relationship with Christ and to discover a ministry they can pour themselves into, the leader must set the example. I'm familiar with a church who hired an "encore" (fifty-plus) pastor based on the fact that he was passionate about living a life of service in his boomer years. Before being hired as the encore pastor, he held a leadership role at a college in the Midwest, but he also spent time every week ministering with nursing home residents. The church leaders felt that his life typified what they wanted to bring about in the lives of other boomers, and so he serves as an example as he seeks to lead others in his same season of life.

Passion also helps the leader be the best advocate for older adults. When a new program or ministry was being discussed at church staff meetings, I would always suggest ways to involve the older adults or what we might do to reach them. The aging boomers and those older deserve an advocate.

A second characteristic of a successful older adult leader is a willingness to learn. All leaders must be learners, but this is one ministry area where that is absolutely essential. The newness of this field and the numerous myths that prevail about aging make it imperative that the leader be constantly gathering information and staying on top of the cultural trends regarding older adults.

Five days a week, I receive an e-mail that includes links to more than thirty news articles regarding aging from all over the world. The academic field of gerontology is growing daily, with more and more colleges and universities including it in their curriculum. Businesses and government organizations are conducting research to better understand the aging baby boomers and the associated challenges and opportunities. Those of us in the church have much we can learn simply by staying on top of the latest discoveries and considering how they affect ministry.

For example, a recent article reported that older adults are the fastest-growing users of Internet dating services and the fastest-growing group of unmarried adults who live together.[3] Some older adults choose to live together rather than marry because of the financial threats that can occur through marriage, such as changes in Social Security status and other retirement income. Other fifty-and-older adults travel together, sharing summer homes and spending weekends together. Just as we teach biblical principles to young people about sex outside of marriage, we will be faced with addressing this same issue among older adults. It's important that we keep up with current aging trends (such as older adults living together) so that we can be effective at understanding and then ministering to this generation.

Reading books, participating in conferences, and attending classes (such as a gerontology course at a local college) are all good avenues for learning about the aging boomer and older adult ministry. But another, often forgotten way to learn is to talk with the older adults themselves. Surveys with the aging boomers in your church and community might be helpful, as would organizing focus groups with this particular age group. When I was first attempting to reach those in the fifty-to-seventy set, I hosted an informal focus group with key people in the church who were in this age range. Over coffee, we discussed some of the primary concerns and pressing issues in their lives. This helped ensure that the goals of the ministry met their needs. It is also good to host groups like this with people from the community who are unchurched. This communicates that we genuinely care about their needs and want to create ministries that will be a blessing to them as well.

The third characteristic, already hinted at, is that the leader needs to be an equipper. Ministry leaders cannot view themselves as doing things *for* older adults but rather as unleashing these people to make a significant impact in their communities. It often seems easier to do things oneself than to be a shepherd or a coach for someone else. I've seen older adult ministries where the leader is visiting the homebound, planning the funeral dinner, teaching the Bible study, organizing the trip, leading the grief support group, and writing the newsletter. This leaves no room for them to lead people to discover their own gifts and use these talents for Kingdom impact. Furthermore, it is impossible for one leader to do all the things that would be valuable and do them effectively. Remember Jethro's advice to Moses in Exodus 18:18 and 21: "What you are doing is not good. . . . The work is too heavy for you, you cannot handle it alone. . . . Select capable men from all the people . . . and appoint them as officials."

## A Designated Leader

By now you might be thinking, "With all this talk about the importance of integrating older adults into the whole church and recognizing that they do not want to be labeled or considered old, should we even have a leader or staff member designated to this area of ministry?" That's a good question. I've wrestled with it myself and have been a part of a number of discussions and meetings addressing this very topic.

There are churches that are working hard to create an environment where every adult is integrated. There is no young adult ministry or singles Sunday school class or senior adult program. These churches don't like putting people into categories. The church staff may have a teaching pastor, a worship pastor, a discipleship pastor, and a missions pastor. And each of these pastors is responsible for bringing about that spiritual practice in the life of every adult. So in theory, the discipleship pastor should be just as passionate about seeing a thirty-year-old growing in faith as seeing an eighty-year-old doing the same. And the worship pastor should be equally interested in leading a sixty-year-old and a twenty-year-old in a meaningful worship experience.

This can be an effective way in which to organize ministry, and it certainly has its benefits. Churches can be laser-focused on their purpose and not get sidetracked with multiple programs and activities. These churches have the potential of creating a family environment where all the generations are regularly interacting and serving alongside one another.

However, there are drawbacks to this approach. Even with an emphasis on including everyone, there may be certain groups of people who get less attention than others. It may be those who need recovery ministries in order to find their way out of the pit and into freedom in Christ; or it may be a specific age group of people who have unique needs and issues that are not being addressed in Bible studies or Sunday sermons. It's hard for a discipleship pastor to keep every life stage as a top priority, and it's hard for adults to feel as if the sermon or Bible study is meant for them when the examples are not at all similar to their own. Life-changing growth as a Christian happens in the daily stuff of our lives. It's when we constantly apply God's Word and His principles to the ups and downs of our lives that we grow in Him.

Having a staff member or church leader who gives full attention to the over-fifty set helps ensure that someone at the church is staying on top of the needs, struggles, and issues of this generation. This does not mean that a church should create yet another program, nor does it mean that other church leaders and staff members do not need to learn about or embrace this particular area of ministry. But by having a designated leader or team that focuses on the aging boomer, fewer people are apt to fall through the cracks.

## Finding the Right Leader

Practically speaking, what should we look for in a leader? Some churches have consistently hired retired pastors who want to slow down or work part time. This can be a risky move. If we want to communicate that the middle and later years of life are a time for active and meaningful service, what does it say when we hire someone who wants to slow down and work less? Many times these retired pastors have old models of older adult ministry in mind. They may plan to spend a few hours each day visiting the seniors in their church and hosting a monthly luncheon.

It is possible for a senior pastor to transition to leading the older adult ministry when he has a passion to see his peers fully engaged in ministry. If a retired pastor catches the vision for reaching and unleashing the aging baby boomers and uses all of his skills of teaching, leading, and motivating, it can be a perfect fit.

Some of the most dynamic older adult ministries I've seen are led by former youth ministers. Good youth ministries are made up of many of the same components that make a good ministry with aging boomers. I'm talking about such things as encouraging people to develop meaningful connections and true biblical community among their peer group, calling people to a cause greater than themselves, engaging people in service and mission opportunities to combat their selfish nature, and discipling people to be fully devoted followers of Christ who sincerely worship Him.

Mark was a student ministries pastor for thirty years before becoming an older adult pastor. As a successful youth pastor, he was passionate about enabling student and adult leaders to release their God-given gifts and talents. His transition into ministry with older adults came when the church began to realize the need for a targeted ministry with older adults. His philosophy of ministry has remained largely unchanged, but now Mark spends his time dreaming about new ways to reach an ever-growing population of adults over fifty. "Many older adults missed the opportunity to know Christ during their teen years; I have a second chance to change the course of their life for eternity."

As the church and society begin to wake up to the aging boomers, more and more Christian colleges and seminaries will need to train students for ministry with older adults. Sometimes we neglect to consider that a young person might be the most suitable leader for this ministry. If the person has a sincere passion for this particular age group, a willingness to learn, and the ability to equip other leaders, it may be well worth the risk.

I'm so thankful that there was a church in Las Vegas willing to step out of the norm and hire me as a twenty-three-year-old in this area of ministry. At first, there was some skepticism among the older adults as to whether a young person could understand their needs and issues. But I took things slowly, working to establish relationships and develop trust. Over time, they embraced and even appreciated my desire to serve alongside them.

This is not an exhaustive list of where to discover a great older adult minister. Ministries can thrive under the leadership of a boomer from the business world. I've also seen a number of dynamic and innovative ministries across the country being led by women as well as former worship pastors and even children's pastors. The key is to find someone who is passionate about reaching this generation, has a teachable spirit, and can train others to lead and serve in the ministry.

Not every church has the capacity to pay for a staff member to specifically lead this group. If that's the case, you should be praying for God to bring a key lay leader and subsequent team to champion this ministry. However, if you are a church that tends to hire staff for particular population segments (women, men, single adults, young adults, and so on), hiring someone for this age group communicates volumes as to the value and importance you place on the ministry. Neglecting to hire someone for this age group when you have ministry staff for nearly every other group immediately communicates what ministries are of higher priority. There's just no way around this.

## Facing Up to Change

Changing and readjusting how we do ministry is never easy. In fact, just changing the way we perceive of older adult ministry is hard work. It requires a paradigm shift. It means thinking of older adults as vital, necessary, and essential components of the church body. It means using everything in our power to launch older adults into meaningful, God-centered work.

Sure, we can continue doing older adult ministry by planning a few trips and having a few luncheons—but a new cohort of older adults will not be reached, and the potential impact to be made for the Kingdom will be lost.

In addition to the ministry changes discussed in this chapter, there are three other essential components we must consider in order to create ministries that will have maximum impact:

service, spiritual growth, and intergenerational health. These components are of paramount importance to the future of older adult ministries, and each of these topics deserves some serious consideration, for without them we will miss the mark in reaching boomers. Each of the next three chapters is devoted to one of these considerations.

# 7

# SERVING

## The Linchpin of a Successful Ministry

If you could somehow look into my soul, you would see that as passionate as I am about every aspect of ministry with older adults, the focus of this chapter on service is one of my most pressing concerns. My lifelong desire is to see older adults fully engaged with God, living significant lives and serving Him wholeheartedly until they take their last breath.

When given the opportunity, I will plead with midlife and older adults that they open their eyes and see how much purpose they still have. That God is not finished with them yet and that their church, their family, their grandkids, their neighborhood, and the world still desperately need them. That we need their experience, their talents, and their unique abilities. I beg them not to "hang it up" because they are retired or because their family thinks they should slow down or because their church no longer asks them to do anything. I ask them to search for a place to serve and to give their lives to God's mission in this world.

While we all want people to be serving God, it's often not as easy as telling them they should do it. And just as we've seen in the areas of retirement, relationships, and physical aging, the new wave of older adults is approaching volunteering differently than older people viewed voluntary service in the past.

## Boomers and Volunteering

Volunteering is typically thought of as doing some kind of unpaid activity that benefits other people. People engage in a variety of volunteer activities, ranging from fundraising for something they consider important to reading books to children at school to cleaning up an elderly person's yard. Over sixty-three million Americans volunteer through or for an organization. Interestingly, one in three of them does so through their church, and many others give their time to schools and educational groups.[1]

While the builder generation was willing to volunteer out of loyalty to the church or an organization, the new generation of older adults (boomers and those slightly older) have different desires when it comes to giving of their time and abilities. This information should not be taken lightly but should alert us to some critical themes that will help us maximize the potential impact of this new generation of older adults.

First, boomers want to do something interesting and challenging. They are ready to jump into a worthwhile cause where they feel they can make a significant social impact.

One of my biggest pet peeves is when we underestimate what older adults can contribute. I've been in numerous churches where a group of five to ten senior adults fold the Sunday worship bulletin, stuff envelopes, and staple newsletters. There is nothing wrong with these activities, and certainly we need people to do these tasks, but age alone is not what makes someone a perfect fit for this role. There are many individuals over the age of fifty who would like to find other ways to contribute to the Kingdom, but too often in the church, we don't think about what those other contributions could be.

For those of us in the church, we've got to answer some questions about our own attitudes. Do we think that once people approach retirement age, they want to (or should) slow down in their serving roles? Or do we challenge people to dream about a community need—such as orphaned children, homelessness, or the unemployed—and ways in which they might draw on their years of experience to make a difference for Christ? Research is finding that adults over fifty-five are willing to volunteer to be the leaders of major efforts in their communities. We must resist buying in to the myth that older adults want to slow down and hand the reins over to someone else.

In addition to volunteering for something challenging, boomers want service opportunities that have a mission. They want to do things that give their lives purpose, meaning, and fulfillment. They want to know their contributions truly matter.

There is no greater mission for older adults to immerse themselves in than the mission of Christ to redeem and heal a broken world. But in some cases, the church is failing to provide older adults with these kinds of opportunities. One man said, "I'm retiring and want to give my time to the church, but I really don't want to be an usher." How sad that older adults are regarded in many churches as useful only as ushers, bulletin folders, and coffee makers. We must give priority to the expansion of volunteer jobs for the aging population. If we don't, these adults will look elsewhere to expend their energy and skills.

In addition to expanding the volunteer jobs, we must also thoroughly explain how their work contributes to God's mission. The work of being an usher or bulletin folder takes on new meaning when people grasp the value of the work. West Side Christian Church in Springfield, Illinois, has volunteers clean and disinfect the toys in the nursery every week. The volunteers are not compelled to serve because they want clean toys; rather they serve because of the mothers who will now attend a church service and be encouraged and challenged in their spiritual walk. Seemingly menial tasks take on new meaning when we help people grasp how the tasks fulfill the mission.

Another important characteristic of fifty-to-seventy-year-old volunteers is that they want to do things on their own terms, usually with short commitments. I've asked retirees to lead certain ministries, and they reply, "I'd like to do that job, but I want to be able to leave town at the drop of a hat" or "I want to travel to see my granddaughter play volleyball" or "I don't want to feel tied down." We need new and innovative ways in which to make best use of the talents of older adults that take their desire for flexibility into account.

Some churches appeal to the boomers' desire for short-term commitments by asking them to serve on ministry teams that will meet for a set amount of time, such as six weeks. They even tell the members of the team they are going to be "fired" after the designated time is over. More often than not, adults are willing to give their time to something when they know there is an end to the project.

A number of churches have birthed their boomer-and-beyond ministries this way. Leaders have asked older boomers to brainstorm about a new ministry for their peers and offer suggestions for starting the ministry. Interestingly, after the six weeks are up, many adults have caught a vision for the ministry and want to keep serving.

Previous generations may have volunteered indefinitely for a program or class, but the unique characteristics of this new generation of older adults have caused some community organizations to rethink how they gain volunteers. Today, more volunteering is centered around specific events, such as giving a week of time to help with the Special Olympics, rather than becoming a member of a club or an association and volunteering with that particular group on an indefinite basis.

Leading-edge boomers are also demonstrating an entrepreneurial spirit, which means they may have their own ideas and dreams for a ministry they would like to invest in. A recent article indicated that over the past decade, Americans between the ages of fifty-five and sixty-four had a higher rate of entrepreneurial activity than any other age group.[2]

George is not quite fifty-five, but he is a boomer and definitely has an entrepreneurial spirit that he is using to do Christ's work among the poor and marginalized in society. He is a highly successful businessman, owning his own mortgage company with branches in a number of cities across the country. A few years ago, on a business trip, he was reading USA Today and was gripped by a story on the prevalence of homelessness. From that time on, his concern continued to grow, and he began to pray about what God would have him do. The result is called the Shelter Fund, and every person who closes a loan is given the opportunity to donate $20 to help with homelessness in the local community. The money is given to homeless ministries in the city where the client lives. Because of George's vision, a significant amount of money has been donated to help people stricken by poverty and unemployment.

An increasing number of leading-edge boomers like George are still working and plan to go on working in some capacity. Yet even as they continue in their careers, these boomers want to give their lives to a worthy cause. When I met Mike, I assumed he was retired because of the amount of time he devoted each week to mentoring high school students. Mike was fifty-eight when he learned about the mentoring program through a chamber of commerce event. He then decided to volunteer and has mentored six students over the past five years. Not only is he helping them with academic skills, but he has also had the opportunity to talk to several students about Christ. Mike told me, "During one of my first visits, the particular student asked me if I was a Christian. For the remaining hour, I told him about my faith and answered many of his questions." It's obvious that Mike is not waiting until his retirement years to make a difference for Christ in the world.

In attempting to understand this new generation of older adults, we must take into consideration the differences in how men and women are approaching retirement and volunteerism. Wrestling with these differences will help us be better prepared to unleash these adults for meaningful ministry.

## Women

When I was in graduate school, I worked part time as the volunteer coordinator for a retirement community. For years, this organization had a volunteer program based largely on groups of women from different churches spending one day a month on the campus filling water pitchers for residents and doing other jobs. There has been tension over the past few years regarding how to get new and younger women to participate. Some people feel that the lack of involvement among this group of women is due to the fact that more women are working today and are therefore unavailable. This assumes that if women were not working, they would be happy to do the volunteer task of filling water pitchers. Interestingly, some academic studies indicate that an increase in work hours among women does *not* result in a decrease of volunteer hours.[3] So what might account for the difficulty in finding volunteers for this particular job?

For one thing, boomer women are different from the women of the preceding generation. For example, boomer women are more interested in doing tasks that allow them to use their specific talents or skills. They are less apt to join a club or group in which they volunteer in a generic capacity and are more likely to carve out a service job that suits their individual goals and allows them to determine when and where they wish to serve.

If we go back to the retirement community example, engaging women volunteers today will more than likely emphasize letting them choose how they want to give of their time, rather than assigning them to predetermined tasks. So an artist may best minister to nursing home residents by going in one evening a week and drawing portraits of the residents. Someone with gardening as a hobby may want to take two Saturdays a month to keep the landscaping at the campus looking nice. You get the idea.

And what about filling the water pitchers? Many women will be suited for this job if they see how it connects to something they personally enjoy, such as visiting individual nursing home residents. As they enter each room to retrieve the water pitcher, they could ask a question that might lead to a meaningful conversation.

It is also important to keep in mind that women who are entering their fifties and sixties are in the process of searching and redefining themselves. This is true whether they have been in the workforce or not.

For many women, their primary role has been to raise children, and they have immersed themselves in this task. As they enter the empty-nest years, they are faced with serious life questions, such as "Who am I?" "What is my purpose now?" and "What is the role I am to play?" Even if women have been in the workforce, as is the case for many boomer women, these questions still arise.

I've observed that women who are fifty to seventy years old have the capacity to be great leaders of Christ-centered church and community efforts, if only someone would empower them to do so.

Kathy is a leading-edge boomer at Chapelwood United Methodist Church in Houston, Texas. The church has a job transition ministry (called JET) to help people who have suffered a job loss and are seeking employment. The ministry had been in existence for a few years when Kathy came on board. She responded to a church announcement asking people to be a part of the vision team to help evaluate and expand the ministry.

Her professional experience as an executive for a corporate search firm has provided valuable insights to the ministry. Under her leadership, the team has developed a Web site as well as a comprehensive plan for walking people through the job-transitioning process. She oversees all facets of the ministry, including the dozen or so job counselors who provide mentoring and encouragement to those coming for help.

## Men

When it comes to retirement, after working long hours in demanding careers, men tend to look forward to less work and more time to relax and be with their spouses. The flip side is that many boomer women are at the peak of their careers. Having taken some time off for child rearing, they are now interested in advancing their careers, pursuing more community involvement, or both.

It is not uncommon for men to retire and women to still be working. This presents both opportunities and challenges for the church. Women tend to volunteer more than men, and yet men who are entering retirement have a unique opportunity to devote large amounts of time to service even without their wives' participation. In a study conducted by VolunteerMatch, almost two-thirds of men over fifty-five said they would like a volunteer opportunity that used their personal or professional skills.[4]

Men need to see a bigger picture for how they can use their time for Kingdom impact. Retired doctors can use their skills as short-term medical missionaries. Those who have been attorneys can give their time to organizations in the community that provide legal services to people who cannot pay. Men good at handyman tasks can use their skills to help widows and single moms with home repair projects.

Bob is a friend of our family's who retired from the Air Force and worked as a full-time volunteer in the worship department at his local church for three and one-half years. He was included in all of the planning meetings, had specific responsibilities, and used his talents and his passion for music to benefit the ministry in a variety of ways. He worked on staging and props, served as the spiritual mentor to the vocalists and band members, and attended all rehearsals in order to give feedback and encouragement. He then spent two years as the director of facilities, again in an unpaid role, using his engineering skills to keep the operation of the building running smoothly. During the five and one-half years he served as a full-time volunteer, his wife continued her work as an elementary school teacher.

The potential to make a mark on society that is available within the older generation is tremendous. As leaders, we have a chance to help people achieve their highest potential for God during the second half of their lives. To make this a reality, we must develop a culture—both corporately as a church and in our interactions with individuals—that inspires all older adults to find their perfect place of service.

## What Churches Can Do to Create a Serving Environment Among Older Adults

There are strategic steps a church can take to create an optimal environment for older adults to envision serving to their greatest potential.

First, *take advantage of every opportunity to tell the stories* of how leading-edge boomers are making a major impact with their lives. Before the start of the all-star major league baseball game in 2009, there was a special program highlighting ordinary people who were serving others in America in extraordinary ways. The video presentation featured a man who sends personalized care packages to soldiers overseas, a woman who knits caps for cancer patients, and a boy with cerebral palsy who raises funds for research on this disease. Interwoven in the presentation were the voices of the five living presidents of the United States, talking about the value of volunteering. At the end of the video, the three community volunteers (along with some others) were led out onto the ball field to be cheered by the thousands of fans and to shake hands with the professional athletes.[5] It was one of those presentations that left you with a lump in your throat and renewed hope that there are people in the world who are doing good.

There is power in a story. That's why Jesus used stories, and that's why some of the best communicators are also great story-tellers. To replace the old paradigm of aging with a new paradigm, we must show people what the new paradigm looks like through real examples. The man I mentioned earlier who said he didn't want to be an usher has a picture in his mind that service in retirement means ushering. It will take a constant flow of new pictures—new stories—to begin to replace that image.

Using video, capturing still photographs, writing stories in your newsletter, having a blog dedicated to the stories of adults making an impact, featuring people on the stage during worship services—all of these are effective methods. Whatever methods we choose, it is critical that we tell the stories often. We want people to see that it is normal and expected for a seventy-year-old to spend three months overseas teaching English as a second language or a sixty-year-old retired executive to be creating a new ministry to help at-risk children in the community. We want all ages of people to begin to realize that this is what the later years of life are all about. We want to create a culture where these people are the rule, not the exception.

A second way for a church to emphasize the worth of older volunteers is to *raise the value of unpaid work*. There is still an undercurrent in our society that believes that a job is more valuable if it is a paying job. But churches and organizations can help change this by viewing certain volunteers as actual staff members, the only difference being they don't receive a paycheck. The volunteers have desks, are given business cards, and are expected to attend meetings. Their opinions are valued, and expectations as to what they must accomplish are high. This type of arrangement empowers people and resonates with the many boomers who indicate that they want to volunteer for leadership roles. Boomers will still want flexibility, to be gone from time to time, but they will take their responsibilities seriously and will find ways to get the work done.

A third step is to *become a church that is intentionally outward focused*. This increases the likelihood of having aging adults engaged in significant ministry. When an attitude of service is embedded in the overall DNA of the church, older adults (as well as people of all ages) are more apt to gravitate toward investing their time in major global and community efforts.

LifeBridge Christian Church in Longmont, Colorado, encourages everyone in the church to participate in serving the community from Thanksgiving to Christmas. The church partners with community organizations on a number of projects, including painting and cleaning a transitional housing facility, assembling and distributing holiday food baskets, and working with the public schools' evening maintenance crews. Well over one thousand adults and children participate in these community service efforts, and many of those involved are adults over the age of fifty.

Often these churchwide service projects lead to older adults serving on a regular basis. John, the coordinator of the handyman ministry at LifeBridge, first became involved in service to the community through the Thanksgiving-to-Christmas churchwide effort. He originally signed up to serve at the local pregnancy center doing handyman work. The experience of giving himself to a worthy cause changed his life. He now leads the handyman ministry at the church, which provides help to widows and the frail elderly. In addition to serving those associated with the church, the ministry has established a relationship with a community organization that refers to them individuals in need of home repair. On average, the handyman ministry serves two or three people every week.

Churches can also *begin challenging people before they reach retirement*. Remember, many boomers and those just slightly older are not planning to retire anytime soon. Yet they have reached a season of life where they have more discretionary time. Many of them can begin taking extended vacations and devote that time to worthy projects. This also is a great way for them to kick the tires, so to speak, and begin thinking about where they want to invest themselves when they do retire.

Each year, Chuck and Marilyn spent their summer vacation traveling to a different continent to explore the land and seek God's direction as to where He wanted them to serve in their retirement years. Sometimes they did this through church-sponsored mission trips, and other times they traveled on their own.

Soon after he retired from his job as an engineer and she retired from hers as a school principal, they went to China. Their desire was to open a mission field in a particular area that was closed at the time to mission work. They had no support system and no privacy, but their perseverance in working with the people paid off. Now, more than fifteen years later, the region is served by pastors, evangelists, medical workers, and even a Christian radio program.

## Leading People to Find Their Place of Service

Some boomers are charting their own course in finding their place to serve, but others need a little guidance. What are some practical things we can do to assist people on their journey to discover the best place for them to use their time and talents?

The first and perhaps most important way we can help people discover a place of service is to *connect them to God so that He can lead them*. Proverbs 16:9 and Jeremiah 10:23 remind us that it is God who directs the steps of a man. While your church might be the best in the whole country at motivating and recruiting volunteers, ultimately, we want people to be serving in the exact spot where God wants them. It is in this place where they will find the most fulfillment and satisfaction and where they will have the most impact. No matter how much we need to fill a slot or find a teacher, we must keep in mind that it is God who draws people to Himself and God who has a unique place in which to use them. One of our primary jobs as leaders is to do all we can to keep people in tune with the Holy Spirit so that God can lead and direct their path.

A few years ago, I met a man named Hal who told me about his work as a volunteer in the Houston prison system for more than fifteen years. When he was sixty years old, he attended church as he typically did each week on Sunday. Sitting in the pew, he heard the familiar words of Jesus from Matthew 25:35–36, "For I was hungry and you gave me something to eat, I was thirsty and you gave me something to drink, I was a stranger and you invited me in, I needed clothes and you clothed me, I was sick and you looked after me, I was in prison and you came to visit me." Hal told me that the words the minister said that morning coincided with something going on in his own soul. God was challenging him to do something that would make a difference in people's lives.

So Hal went looking for a way to serve prison inmates in Houston. He agreed to go through an extensive training program that culminated in his participating as a one-on-one mentor to inmates. He faithfully met with men once a week to visit, study the Bible, and pray with those that most of society had forgotten.

As Hal grew older, the drive downtown each week became too much, so he shifted his ministry to prisoners in Sugarland, Texas, which was closer to his home. When I first talked to Hal, he was seventy-seven years old and still mentoring these men. There were times when he gave his own money to hire attorneys for inmates, built relationships with family members, and patiently encouraged, prayed, and waited on the Lord. Many of the men he now counts as friends, and he stays in touch with them even after they are released from prison.

Hal's entry into this powerful ministry came as he listened to the prompting of the Holy Spirit. Through the words of a sermon in which the minister preached the truths of Scripture, God was able to move Hal into the place of service designed uniquely for him.

Helping people stay in step with God doesn't only come through preaching and teaching; it also happens as we pray for people and encourage them to share what they are gleaning from their daily reading of the Bible.

This runs into a second way of helping people find a place of service, which is to *be intentional about discipling older adults*.

Recently, I was invited to be a part of a leadership team with a church denomination that is charting a course for an encore (fifty-plus) ministry. During our first meeting, there was much discussion about how to get members of the boomer generation involved in meaningful service for others. One man on our team whispered to me, "Could their lack of involvement be the result of years of poor discipleship?" His words resonated with something that had been brewing inside of me for quite a while.

Christ-centered serving grows out of a genuine relationship with God. When we are abiding with Him, listening to Him, surrendering to Him, and obeying Him, the natural by-product is that we will bear fruit (John 15). The fruit should be that we worry less, love people more, and take a greater interest in the things that are eternal rather than temporal. It should also increase our compassion for people and our longing to serve them just as Christ has served us.

Wendell Nelson, pastor of spiritual formation at Christ Community Church in Omaha, Nebraska, believes in the importance of developing a strong spiritual foundation in individual lives. He leads a ministry where people grow in Christ-likeness by being a part of a gender-specific group of three people who are similar in age. These small numbers allow each of the members to dive deeply into what has formed and shaped their faith and how God is leading them today.

Wendell encourages each participant to chart his or her faith journey and identify the significant spiritual markers that indicate where God was working. As is often the case, a crisis or trial becomes a marker for God's doing something transformational in a person's life. Scott is a fifty-four-year-old pharmaceutical rep who had some serious health problems that caused him to wrestle with his own mortality. As a result of openly sharing this struggle, praying about it with the other men, and allowing God to work on him, he began to discover that he wanted to do something of significance for God's Kingdom. His love of football led him to begin a Fellowship of Christian Athletes chapter in his home, where he hosts as many as seventy high school boys in his basement twice a month. Many of the boys do not have fathers who are involved in their lives, and Scott has become a father figure to them. Some of the young people are coming to Christ, and even some of the parents have made a decision to surrender their lives to God.

I have met with three men who were in one of Wendell's groups. All three are in their fifties or sixties, and all three are using their lives to make a significant impact for God's Kingdom. Discipleship matters.

A third method for helping people find their unique place is to *encourage them to serve in an area where they've always had an interest*. For many adults, as they age and have more discretionary time, they choose to participate in things they did not have time for when they had children at home and the demands of work and other responsibilities. I've talked with older adults who have started quilting, painting, and golfing in the middle and later years of their lives. Ministry should be no different. This season of life can be the perfect time for adults to work in an area where they have an interest but never had the opportunity.

Bobbie had always had a desire to go on a mission trip, and yet the chance to do so did not present itself until she was eighty years old. Fortunately, she did not let age deter her from participating in a trip with her church to a country in Central America where she prayed with the people there, held and comforted babies, and encouraged the women who lived in the region to stay close to the Lord. She was a tremendous blessing to the people who lived there as well as an inspiration to the mission team. She never complained about the heat or the uncomfortable accommodations but was simply grateful for the opportunity to serve.

People say they volunteer because they want to help people or get involved or stay busy or make a difference, but most often the work they do is a specific task, such as rocking babies, raising funds, or building a house. The job itself may have sparked their interest, making them realize it was something they'd always wanted to do and now had the time to do.

A close cousin to appealing to their interests is to *provide adults with exposure to ministry opportunities*. Short-term mission trips can be a great way for people over fifty to discover the one thing they want to invest themselves in. Northshore Baptist Church in Bothell, Washington, has sent numerous mission teams to Los Cedros, Nicaragua. Sometimes the retirees that go on one mission trip will return to spend more time on a certain project. Jack and Katie went on a trip with the church and were so troubled by the needs of the people that they returned on their own and spent an entire month in the community in order to forge business partnerships. For the community to sustain itself, there must be jobs for the people. Because of this, Jack felt compelled to use his own business experience to help set up possible employment opportunities in the community.

Exposure can come in other forms besides mission trips. The Boomer Plus ministry at Calvary Assembly Church in Winter Park, Florida, spearheaded a ministry called ARK (Acts of Random Kindness). First the ministry team drew up a list of twenty-five ideas for serving the community, such as working with a residential program for troubled boys and girls, providing respite care for families with special-needs children, or creating and sending cards to the sick. The boomer ministry then hosted Community Fest, an evening when anyone in the church could come and be introduced to these ministries. Each ministry was given a room in the church, and a facilitator was present to write down the names of individuals interested in serving and how they might be involved. Many of the adults would not have thought about serving in one of the twenty-five areas had they not been presented with the ministry.

Another way of providing guidance is to *show older adults how they might use their past work experiences* as tools for ministry. For many people, the skills they used in their career can now be channeled into meaningful Kingdom work.

My father was a successful accountant for a large oil company before retiring. He now spends eight to ten hours every week as the volunteer financial director for the local Habitat for Humanity chapter. His attention to detail and ability to manage multiple projects are assets to the organization. Before he retired, he thought that working with Habitat would appeal to him, and he assumed that his work would involve swinging a hammer. Little did he know that God had a task carved out that would specifically use his unique abilities and experience.

An extremely important way of directing people is to *tap in to their passion*. When we first moved to Nebraska, I could not get over how fanatical people were about Husker football. No events or classes were scheduled at the church without first consulting the dates for the football games. People who were planning to get married in the fall worked their wedding dates around the games. It seemed crazy to me, but I've come to learn that Nebraska is not the only place where this happens. All across the country, there are sports fans who are passionate about their teams.

Passion is what stirs people deep in their soul and gives them a single focus. It's the stuff that we will talk about with anyone who will listen and the stuff that keeps us awake at night as we dream about it.

I like the definition Bruce Bugbee uses for passion when he says it is "the God-given desire that compels us to make a difference in a particular ministry."[6] It's that one thing we feel we must do. James Dobson's passion for the family resulted in the birth of Focus on the Family. Everett Swanson's passion for orphaned children became the beginning of Compassion International.

For some people, their passion is obvious. You only have to be around them a few minutes before you can pick up on it. I wear my passion for older adult ministry on my sleeve. Often I've had people say, "You just come alive when you start talking about this," or "Your eyes light up and you are so animated about this subject." Early on in my ministry, those remarks reassured me that I was on the right path in doing the work God had for me to do.

With other people, it can take some time to help them identify their passion and especially how they might use that passion as ministry for God's Kingdom. That brings me to a seventh suggestion. You must *have intentional conversations and in those conversations be a good listener.* It sounds so basic, and yet we often do not do it.

As you talk to others, you want to listen for the things they care about. You may hear them talk about their fishing expeditions, their love of quilting, or their mother's cancer treatments. Ministry can be developed through all three of these things. Hospice programs and nursing homes often have volunteers who have been on the receiving end of these services. The way they were helped and the value they found in the organization gives them a compelling reason to serve in this area. Those who like to fish can use the sport to build relationships with non-Christians. A number of churches have quilting ministries where quilt lovers gather to sew prayer quilts for people who are suffering from cancer or another illness.

It can also be useful to *direct people to a spiritual gifts inventory and other assessments* that help them identify who they are and what they are good at. The key is to go beyond the inventory. Kevin Burdette, the minister of Adult Impact at Green Acres Baptist Church in Tyler, Texas, was approached by a married couple in their early fifties who said they were bored. The man had sold his oil and gas business and the woman had sold her hair salon, and they wanted something meaningful to do with their time. Kevin asked them to take an online spiritual gifts assessment and e-mail him the results. Then he had a face-to-face meeting with them in order to get to know them and draw out of them what they both love to do. He then told them to spend the next three weeks roaming the halls of the children's ministry just to observe. He also put them in touch with the Christian Women's Job Corps and the Christian Men's Job Corps. Today, the woman is serving with a children's apartment ministry and the man is continuing to explore various possibilities. Their journey to find a place to serve began with talking with a trusted leader and then assessing how God had uniquely wired them.

Personality tests, learning style inventories, and a host of other resources are available to assist adults in discovering who they are and where they might like to serve. Sometimes the best assessments come in the form of a few questions.

Ken Dychtwald and Dan Kadlec suggest that aging boomers consider certain questions in their quest to find what's next for them in life.[7] A colleague of mine modified a couple of these to be more appropriate for a ministry context. It is an easy exercise that should take less than twenty minutes to complete.

- Make a list of every job you have ever had and what you loved about it.
- Create a similar list of your ministry and volunteer pursuits and what you loved about them.
- Write down some of your childhood dreams.
- Document how you have spent your discretionary income.
- Ask family and friends to describe moments in life when you seemed happiest.
- Identify how you are using or not using the things you've written down for Kingdom work.

The key to any type of assessment, questionnaire, or exercise is what happens after it is completed. Intentional conversations that help people verbalize who they are, what they've discovered about themselves, and what they care about are essential in moving them toward a significant ministry.

A word of caution is warranted here. For this to be effective, we as leaders cannot view people as simply bodies that can fill empty slots at church. Instead, by considering their spiritual gifts, their passion, and their experience, we can point them in a direction where they can discover the perfect fit for themselves.

## Jesus: The Model Servant

The topic of serving has been woven into nearly every chapter of this book, and its importance in building a ministry with aging baby boomers cannot be overemphasized. Boomers want to make a major impact with their remaining years of life, and the church needs to help harness their capacity for the greatest influence. But ultimately, for the Christian, servanthood should be a life-style. A lifestyle of imitating Christ. And while we need to do everything we can to help people find their sweet spot where they can expend themselves toward a worthy cause, this doesn't take away the importance of their performing daily acts of service. We want adults to be servants who are more than willing to do the mundane tasks, the ordinary jobs that communicate love and care to others.

When I was doing research for my doctoral dissertation on volunteerism, I came across two descriptions of volunteering. The first was *formal volunteering*, which best describes what we've talked about throughout most of this chapter. Formal volunteering usually comes from working with an organization and giving time to a specific task: rocking babies in a hospital, collecting donations for the poor, organizing a campaign against domestic violence. *Informal volunteering* is what we do in our daily lives to help others: watering a neighbor's plants, cooking a meal for a friend who has been sick, meeting with a colleague whose marriage is struggling. Interestingly, studies have found that people who do more informal helping also tend to be involved in more formal volunteering activities.[8]

As we help people find the big ways God can use them, we must encourage them to have their eyes open to where they can be a servant every day. In my own life, there have been too many times when I'm late to an "important" ministry task and I don't stop to talk with my neighbor whose sister was diagnosed with an illness or pause to speak a kind word to my husband before rushing out the door. Those things are just as much a part of serving as the structured task. Serving people is what we are called to do even if it is not marked on the calendar with a specific time and place.

Jesus accomplished his mission. He taught people the good news and led them to the Father. But he also had time for the individual needs of people—to sit with children, to spend time with the sick, to hang out with His disciples, even to serve His disciples, His closest friends, as we see best in John 13:3–5: "Jesus knew that the Father had put all things under his power, and that he had come from God and was returning to God; so he got up from the meal, took off his outer clothing, and wrapped a towel around his waist. After that, he poured water into a basin and began to wash his disciples' feet, drying them with the towel that was wrapped around him."

Both types of service are important for the aging baby boomer: the formal and the informal, the organized and the moment-by-moment. They work in tandem. And they are both worthy of our time and effort.

Engaging older adults to make a major impact for Christ in the world should be a primary foundation for ministry with boomers—if not *the* primary foundation. We have an open window of time right now to help individuals in midlife and older refocus their priorities and recognize how God wants to use them for His purposes in this season of their lives. Let's not miss the chance.

# 8

# MATTERS OF FAITH

## Spiritual Growth for the Boomer

Over the past fifteen years, the study of spirituality and aging has become a respected area of discussion in the academic world. Duke University, the University of Chicago, and Baylor University are just a few of the educational institutions that support faculty and fund research on this topic. Every year, numerous academic articles are written, dissertations are published, and research is conducted on spirituality and aging.

Topics of study in this area range from the impact of religion on health as people age to the life satisfaction of older adults who participate in religious activities. Sometimes an aging conference will have a specialized track on spirituality, and the workshops in this area might include the benefits of meditation for an older adult or using t'ai-chi as a spiritual exercise.

But these classes and presentations always leave me empty and wanting more. While recognizing that religion has its benefits, my desire is not to have people's physical health improve because they go to church or for them to feel happier because they read a daily spiritual poem. Rather I want to see older adults truly living a life of complete and full devotion to Jesus Christ, right until the moment they take their last breath. I bet many of you have this same desire.

Helping older adults grow in spiritual maturity like this does not happen automatically. It's a lot harder than sending someone to one class or workshop. It starts with identifying and letting go of the myths of aging that keep us from spiritually investing in the lives of aging adults. Myths like "older adults are already

Christians," "older adults can't change," and "older adults are wise and spiritually mature." Those myths hinder people from growing in their faith. Middle-age and older adults need intentional love and discipleship, just as teenagers and young adults do. And they are worth our time and effort. As long as an individual is breathing, God is working. God is constantly seeking to draw people closer to Himself and mold them to be more like Christ.

Of course, this looks different for every person. Some adults have little to no relationship with God and have never named Him as their Savior. Others need to "grow up in their faith" and learn what it means to live every day surrendered to the Holy Spirit.

People never reach a point where they can choose to stop growing in their faith. And while the Holy Spirit is constantly working in the lives of individuals in different ways and through different circumstances, there are some key areas we should pay attention to as we minister with boomers.

## Evangelism

A few months ago, I read an extremely sad news article, the kind where you finish reading and sit completely still because you are absolutely stunned. It was about an older couple from Britain who traveled to Switzerland in order to die together at an assisted suicide clinic. The wife was diagnosed with cancer and given not much time to live. The husband simply wasn't able to live the quality of life he desired and wanted to die with his wife. The article said they both calmly drank the lethal barbiturate and lay down, holding hands as their lives slipped away. At the end of the article, a short sentence said the couple was not religious and there would be no funeral.

I kept staring at the couple's picture, thinking that more than likely, this man and woman did not know Christ as their Savior and were now lost for eternity. It was a startling reminder that not all older adults are Christians.

## Myth: Older Adults Are Already Christians

Not all stories sound as tragic as that of this European couple, and yet there are older adults all around us who are without Christ.

Reaching out and loving older adults who have not yet surrendered their lives to Jesus should be a critical component of ministry with aging adults. Yet despite the growth of the older population and the number of older adults who are not Christians, churches by and large are spending most of their energy and resources reaching out to young adults. This may be because church leaders believe that older adults are already religious.

At the beginning of each semester, I have my college students take a quiz regarding twenty-five common myths of aging—myths like those mentioned in Chapter Two, such as old people lose their memory, old people can't learn new things, and old people are religious. Throughout the years of giving this quiz, the myth of older adults' being religious is one of the most frequently missed questions. Students equate the conservative nature of some older adults and their disapproval of younger generations' lifestyle choices as indicators that older adults are religious. Some students simply think that being old makes people religious.

Regardless of what we (or others) may believe, the truth is that there are many older adults who do not know Christ. Just a few days ago, my husband conducted a funeral service for a seventy-one-year-old man who had no religious background—nor did his wife or the rest of the family.

There are also older adults who may have gone to church when they were young and even made a decision to follow Christ, but faith has not been a part of their lives for many years. Community Christian Church, a multisite church in Naperville, Illinois, has a site at Carillon, a fifty-five plus living community. The church's mission is "helping people find their way back to God." This statement is a great description of both the evangelistic work and spiritual growth efforts we should strive for with boomers and those who are older.

## Myth: Older Adults Can't Change

A second myth that keeps church leaders from pursuing evangelistic efforts with older adults is an underlying belief that older
adults are stuck in their ways and can't change. We may think
that if someone has reached the age of fifty, sixty, or seventy and
is not yet a follower of Christ, there won't be much chance of
their coming to faith. Or perhaps we think there is not enough
time to convince them. Yet Scripture paints an entirely different
picture (emphasis added):

> "*Everyone* who calls on the name of the Lord will be saved"
> (Romans 10:13).

> "[The Lord] is patient with you, not wanting anyone to
> perish, but *everyone* to come to repentance" (2 Peter 3:9).

> "For the Son of Man came to seek and to save what was
> *lost*" (Luke 19:10).

> "He said to them, 'Go into all the world and preach the
> good news to *all creation*'" (Mark 16:15).

> "God . . . wants *all men* to be saved and to come to a
> knowledge of the truth" (1 Timothy 2:3–4).

God's heart—his mission—has always been to redeem people.
Regardless of gender, race, socioeconomic status, or age. He
never puts an age qualifier on who is worthy of salvation, and
neither should we. If we believe that older adults can't change
and therefore are not worth our time, money, and effort, we are
essentially putting a limit on what we believe God can do. God
has always been in the business of changing people's lives. Age
is no exception to this.

A few years ago, I received a newsletter telling the story of
an eighty-five-year-old Buddhist monk who took off his Buddhist
robe and entered a stream to be baptized and surrender his life
to Christ. I've talked to pastors who have witnessed adults in

their sixties, seventies, and eighties whose lives have been radically changed as they've accepted the message of salvation. With God, change is always possible.

## Are Older Adults Receptive?

Nearly a decade ago, George Barna reported that people over the age of fifty were one of three groups discovered to be the most receptive to the gospel message.[1] And there is no reason to believe that this research does not still hold true today. There are some fundamental reasons why adults in the middle and later years of life are responsive to the message of the gospel.

Most textbooks on aging will point out that older adulthood is a season of significant life change. A number of transitions, losses, and potential crises are commonly experienced by individuals in this particular stage of life. Retirement, health changes in self or a family member, the death of close friends and family members, and new living arrangements are just a few of the many challenges affecting aging boomers. It is widely accepted that during periods of stress and crisis, people are more responsive to religion. Harold Koenig, a leading researcher in the field of aging, suggests a reason for this: "In order for God to become the object of a person's ultimate concern (as occurs in true religious conversion), the possession, person, or goal that previously served this purpose (of being the ultimate concern) must be displaced. This displacement often occurs through loss (of a loved one through death/divorce, loss of a career goal through failure of a business, or loss of independence or physical prowess through illness)."[2]

Research also shows that adults who turn to religion in times of crisis have had some religious background, even if they have been away from it for many years. We cannot underestimate the importance of being ready and available to listen, encourage, and lead aging boomers to Christ as they move into the later years of life.

A second reason boomers may be open to matters of faith is because of their quest to find meaning and purpose.

The movie *About Schmidt* tells about a man named Warren Schmidt who retires from his corporate job and struggles to discover who he is at this stage in his life. Early on in the film, you find him flipping channels on the television, going back to the office to offer his help, doing a crossword puzzle, and having breakfast with his wife in their new RV. None of these scenes depict Warren as being very happy or content. Rather you get the strong impression that he is searching for his purpose.

For many boomers, purpose has been found through career, family, the accumulation of money and things, and even the pursuit of hobbies and leisure activities. As they begin to enter into the second half of life, they are evaluating if these things really provide lasting fulfillment. Retirement, the empty nest, and health issues can all be reasons for rethinking what brings meaning to life.

Purpose, as we've already seen, is a major theme in the lives of middle-age and older adults. A number of initiatives are occurring encouraging boomers to volunteer or begin new careers that will focus on community service. In 2009, President Barack Obama signed the Service America Act, which encourages public service among middle-age adults.[3] New books on the market are calling older adults to give of their time and expertise in ways that will make a difference in the lives of other people.

Serving others and giving oneself to a worthy cause are among the primary ways boomers are finding purpose. Some older adults looking for something meaningful to do may be drawn to the church because of a certain service project in which the church is involved. They may have a passion for this particular project and start to volunteer. And over time, they begin to recognize the one thing that provides lasting purpose: a relationship with Jesus Christ.

Volunteering for an important effort or devoting hours each week to making a difference in the community will not provide the deep, abiding purpose people are searching for. Real purpose begins with recognizing God as the ultimate purpose giver. And then, as an extension of the meaning and purpose found through Him, opportunities to serve others for His glory become even more meaningful.

A third reason adults come to Christ in their later years is because of their desire for meaningful relationships. Relationships change as people age. I've already pointed out some of these changes, including children moving away, aging parents needing more care, retirement altering relationships with coworkers and old friends, and the death of family members. New relationships are necessary but sometimes hard to find. The church can be a primary place of social interaction where people can connect with one another and talk about life issues.

All three of these factors—help dealing with life's changes, a search for purpose, and a desire for meaningful relationships—can powerfully work together in drawing older adults to Christ's saving grace.

Dowe was an older man who came to the church where my husband and I served when his wife was dying. Frankly, he was looking for a pastor who would perform her funeral service. His interaction with the pastor who conducted the service and his own grief process led him to begin attending some church activities. He was lonely, and church became a place for him to find friends. As time went on, this retired man began to find purpose by serving at the church. He involved himself in the visitation ministry and was willing to help with the set-up and tear-down of events. He started attending Bible studies and other church activities and eventually reached a point where he made a formal decision to surrender his life to Christ and be baptized. He was nearly eighty years old at this time.

Crisis, meaningful relationships, a sense of purpose—the Holy Spirit used all three of these needs to draw this man to God.

## Making It Happen

Recognizing the need to reach older adults for Christ and realizing their receptivity is important, but even more critical is making evangelism a reality. In my interaction with various churches and leaders, I've discovered a few key methods for reaching boomer adults.

One effective way of bringing older adults into a relationship with Christ is through a *small group ministry*. There are a number of church-affiliated small groups within Carillon the fifty-five-plus community I mentioned earlier. And while these groups have a component of Bible study, the emphasis is on building relationships. The church members who live in the community believe in the value of small groups and friendship evangelism. Loren is a retiree who lives in Carillon and is a small group leader sold out to the vision of loving his peers. He told me how many of the group's friends and neighbors have come to Christ: "Basically, a non-Christian is invited to one of our groups and gets to know people. The newcomer may do things one-on-one with other group members, such as shopping or playing shuffleboard, and slowly over months, the person builds a relationship. Each week, the person comes to the small group and is studying the Bible and hearing other people talk about the lessons and in turn begins to get excited about God."

A second method is *hanging out in the places where older adults gather*. Don't assume that all older adults are already going to church. They are not. We need to go to where they are and love them in their environment.

Rod Toews is an older adult pastor at Peninsula Covenant Church in Redwood City, California, who wants to see fifty-plus-age adults from the church involved as members in every social club in the geographical area that surrounds the church. Rod has taken the lead by becoming a member of the Redwood City Rotary Club. He encourages his people not just to join as members but to actively participate. Rod told me that he has been more involved in one-on-one evangelism through this club than he's ever been in his life. He even had the opportunity to conduct the funeral service for the wife of one of the club members, and since then the husband has been regularly attending the church. Rod constantly keeps the vision in front of his older adults by frequently showing them a roster of all the clubs in the area and encouraging them to get involved.

Health centers, RV clubs, and Starbucks are all potential venues for building relationships with aging boomers who are unbelievers. Even volunteering in the community will afford the opportunity to meet older adults who are volunteers.

A third way to reach boomer adults is to host *events that appeal to boomers' interests and needs*. Stu and Kathy initially knew of LifeBridge Christian Church in Longmont, Colorado, because their grandson was involved in the church preschool. While Kathy, who is fifty-nine, had some church background, Stu, who is sixty-eight, had never gone to church. Through an advertisement, he saw that the fifty-and-over adults were going on a ski trip, and he signed up to go. After a positive and enjoyable experience, he started participating in the fifty-plus ministries bike trips and having significant conversations with other people. He and his wife later decided to join a small group Bible study with other adults in their season of life. The leader of the group, also an older adult, invested in Stu, answering his questions and taking an interest in his life. It wasn't long after that Stu made a decision to commit his life to Christ. Since then, both he and his wife have become leaders on the Prime Time team, a ministry devoted to planning events that reach out to adults age fifty to sixty-five.

Inviting boomers to get involved in *service opportunities* is another entry point for their finding God. Because we know that older adults are searching for ways to make a significant impact, we can encourage them to help with community projects and in turn give them the opportunity to rub shoulders with Christians who care about the same causes they do.

Harold is a retired man and a strong Christian who attends First Baptist Church in Mountain Home, Arkansas. Harold regularly volunteered at the local hospital, where he met Jim, also a volunteer. In fact, Jim spent forty to sixty hours every week doing various tasks at the hospital. As Harold and Jim served together, a friendship grew, and Harold introduced Jim to the older adult pastor at the church. Soon thereafter, Jim made the decision to follow Christ and be baptized. He has become more involved at church, making friends and getting involved in Bible studies.

I have a friend who volunteers with some other men from his church in an organization that moves women and children who are at risk of harm into safe housing. One of the social workers with this organization has anti-Christian bumper stickers on her car and yet has been profoundly affected by the ministry these men provide. Nearly every time they help with a move, one or two of the guys have significant conversations with her about why they serve and the kind of church they attend.

This woman and these men from the church both care about people affected by domestic violence, and this common ground gives them the opportunity to have spiritual conversations about Jesus and church. Hopefully, this will one day lead her into a relationship with the Lord.

## Discipleship

Just as it is important we acknowledge that not all older adults have a relationship with Christ, it is equally important to know not all older Christians are mature in their faith.

### Myth: Older Adults Are Wise and Spiritually Mature

A positive stereotype often attached to older individuals is that they are wise and spiritually mature. Certainly, age can bring wisdom. Many leading-edge boomers have a wealth of life experience that makes them good leaders, teachers, counselors, and advisers for a church. However, not all adults who are past the age of fifty are particularly wise. Some older adults should not be leading or teaching young people because they themselves are still living as spiritual babes (Hebrews 5:12).

All churches have adults who have attended church for most of their lives. They may serve in some capacity and even participate in Bible studies, but they seem to be unchanged in terms of how they live and relate to people. Their lives do not exhibit the fruit of the Spirit, nor do they live as mature followers of Christ.

Every single one of us has weaknesses, places where we want (and need) to grow. We regularly feel like Paul when he says in Romans 7:15, "I do not understand what I do. For what I want to do I do not do, but what I hate I do." The goal is that we learn to surrender daily to the Holy Spirit and allow Him to change us.

Personally, I hope that people who know me now will be able to say of me in ten years, "Amy is more loving, less critical, and worries less." Those are some of the spiritual areas where God is working on me. I pray about these issues, memorize and meditate on Scripture as it relates to these, and share my setbacks and successes with a few Christian friends.

Older adults also have areas where they need to grow, and as leaders, we should be aware of some of these sins that can be spiritual pitfalls for those in mid and late life.

*Materialism*   The drive to make the most money we can and then spend that money on things that make us happy is very prevalent in our culture. It has been a primary goal and objective of many of the leading-edge boomers. They have worked hard at their careers and have wanted to have the best cars, homes, and toys. They've been conditioned to save for retirement and now to spend this money on pleasures for themselves. Older adults need to be challenged not to set their minds on earthly things but rather to be focused on things above (Colossians 3:2). They need encouragement to give their money and use the things they have accumulated for God's glory. This might be offering a room in their home for a missionary or church intern or sharing their finances with ministries that are making a difference. In whatever way people give, the point is to develop a deeper dependence on God and recognize that everything belongs to Him.

*Selfishness* Living an unselfish life is hard, but it is the life Christ calls us to. A self-centered heart is apparent when we demand that things go our way. Perhaps you've heard some of these statements: "Church should play the music I like"; "The doctor should see me when I want to be seen"; "The kids should visit me more often." Some older adults believe they have earned the right to these and other things because of their age, but this attitude is definitely not biblical. Jesus says, "If anyone would come after me, he must *deny himself*" (Matthew 16:24, emphasis added). It doesn't get much clearer than that. Christ followers of any age must lay down what they perceive to be their rights and take up the selfless attitude of Christ.

I serve on a national Christian ministry's board of directors with a retired physician who is seventy years old. As I've become friends with this fascinating man, I've learned that he regularly takes mission trips where he can use his skills as a physician to minister with people who cannot receive the care we do in the United States.

The last time I was with him, I asked him about his latest work and ministry. After he told me of his recent mission trip to Mexico, he said, "Amy, so many of the people in my church, who are my age, are amazed at what I do. But the reality is they could be doing it too. The problem is they have taken on a consumer mentality, even as Christians, even in the church."

Not many of us would want to be associated with the word *consume*. In fact, the dictionary defines *consume* as "to destroy or expend by use; to devour." So a consumer is someone who devours and uses up without giving anything back. In other words, consumers are selfish. They care only about themselves and what they are receiving.

Aging adults with a self-centered mentality must be confronted and challenged to live a life that puts others' needs above their own. I've been blessed to experience this firsthand as I've interacted with older adults all over the country. They are gracious and flexible when things don't go as originally planned, and they've been an example to me. One Sunday, I had a speaking engagement at a church about two and one-half hours from our home. Upon waking in the morning, I discovered our daughter had a fever and was sick. She couldn't go with my husband to the retirement community where he conducted church services, nor could she go with me. Fortunately, Grandma (who lives an hour away) was able to babysit, but to coordinate schedules, I would have to arrive at the church later than planned. When I called, the people were so accommodating and flexible. Situations like this have happened to me over and over again and probably to you as well. As I watch the response of older adults in these circumstances, I am learning what it means to get the focus off myself and onto someone else. Older adults who lead unselfish lives serve as a model to the people around them.

**Idolatry** It's a touchy subject, but we must recognize that family members can actually become idols. An idol is anything we set up as being greater than God, and aging boomers are at risk of making grandchildren and even adult children into idols. Sometimes overinvolvement with grandchildren and family keeps people from seeking God, attending church, or serving in ministry.

I'm not saying that it is essential for people to be in a church building every single Sunday in order to be right with God, nor do I believe that all adults should leave their grandchildren and move overseas to work in the mission field. In fact, a primary ministry for grandparents *is* their family. Grandparents can spiritually invest in their grandchildren and even lead them to Christ.

They can serve their adult children by offering them financial help as well as child care and domestic support. I've personally benefited from this type of ministry throughout this past year. I would not have been able to devote the time necessary to write this book if it weren't for my parents and in-laws, who were willing to provide babysitting for our children.

It is not all or nothing. People can be active with their grand-children and still put God first. But some adults need to be challenged to evaluate their lives and ensure that God and His desires take precedence above everything and everyone else.

Kay Warren, a baby boomer and wife of Rick Warren, pastor of Saddleback Church in Lake Forest, California, was gripped by God to do something about the worldwide HIV/AIDS epidemic. She travels, speaks, and serves as an advocate for people with HIV/AIDS. She's gone from being a stay-at-home mom to being in full-time ministry. In her book *Dangerous Surrender*, she writes about the ramifications this has had on her family:

> It has been a painful time for everyone. We have spent hours and hours sharing with each other and listening to each other's fears, concerns, worries, and even grief. My precious daughter, Amy, was at the stage of life when she was having children, and she wanted me around to share in these experiences on a daily basis. She was used to my being readily available. One day she poured out her heart and said, "I miss you, Mom. I see other grandmothers going to the park with their grandkids every week—they're available to go to lunch with their daughter at a moment's notice, they go shopping together, they hang out, and I wanted that for us."[4]

Kay goes on to say that when she cuddles her granddaughter, she also thinks of those abandoned babies left in a field. She sees the faces of abused little girls and hurts for the children who are looking for food in garbage dumps. Kay says, "Surely God can enable us to care for both our own families and those who have no family."[5] In no way does Kay's work mean that she has left her family or loves them less. She still spends time with her husband and children and cares deeply for each one of them. But she listened to God and put Him first.

The bottom line is to not make people (even grandkids) more important than God and the work He wants to do in and through us. From time to time, we may need to be the voice to give older adults this reminder.

**Squandering Talents and Experience**   Scripture is clear that Christians need to be good stewards of the gifts and talents God has given them. Not only is this applicable to adults giving their finances for Kingdom work, but it also applies to how we spend our time and use our abilities. Aging adults who have the attitude that they have paid their dues and now it is time for the younger ones to serve are going against what Jesus teaches.

In the parable of the talents in Matthew 25, Jesus says it is important to invest what we've been given. By the time Christians are fifty or sixty years old, they have been given much, including experience, knowledge, and abilities. Some older adults have gifts of organization and can arrange a food drive for the community or a children's program for underprivileged kids. Over the years, some adults have refined their leadership abilities and are capable of spearheading important ministry projects. I read about one man who worked with his pastor to lead a major community outreach to show the movie *The Passion of the Christ* when it was released.[6]

Using our gifts and abilities to invest our lives as Jesus commands is not always easy. It may involve taking a risk. For older adults, these risks might include moving overseas for a year to teach English, befriending someone of a different race, or becoming a foster parent or grandparent.

Perhaps one of the most risky things for older boomers is to allow God to use their own difficult life experiences to help someone else. Some adults have cared for a parent suffering with Alzheimer's disease, and they could now be a source of strength to someone in the same situation. Or they know what it is like to have an adult child who has rejected faith in Christ, and they could provide love and hope to someone else. Unfortunately, many older adults don't want to talk about the difficult times in their lives.

It is imperative that we help adults over the age of fifty see how their trials and sorrows could be used in a powerful way to minister to others. This is the message of 2 Corinthians 1:3–4, "Praise be to the God and Father of our Lord Jesus Christ, the Father of compassion and the God of all comfort, who comforts us in all our troubles, so that we can comfort those in any trouble with the comfort we ourselves have received from God."

Whatever the actual ministry, leading-edge boomers have something to offer others. Adults should not waste their gifts, abilities, and life experiences but rather should use them to make a significant impact for Christ in this world.

**Fear and Anxiety** There are a lot of things to worry about as a person ages. Changes in health, the welfare of adult children and grandchildren, the loss of loved ones, and one's own death are just a few of the concerns facing aging boomers. Worry can paralyze people and keep them from living the abundant life God has intended.

Aging boomers who are Christians must be reminded that fear signals a lack of trust in God and His sovereign will. We can help adults learn to recognize fear as a sin and then teach them to put God's Word into practice.

"Do not be anxious about anything, but in everything, by prayer and petition, with thanksgiving, present your requests to God. And the peace of God which transcends all understanding, will guard your hearts and your minds in Christ Jesus" (Philippians 4:6–7). I can remember the difficult circumstances in my own life when I began to practice this verse. I would wake in the middle of the night, gripped with worry, and would begin to pour out my anxiety to God, thank Him, ask Him for the desire of my heart, and then focus on the peace He would provide. I am in no way perfect at doing this, but I'm beginning to learn what it means to believe God's Word to such an extent that I will act on what He says.

Another way to help people with fear is to teach them to dwell on the things of God rather than on their worries. A tangible way to do this is to ask older adults in a small group setting to write down the things we are to think about listed in Philippians 4:8 and then to share with one another how they will practically turn their thoughts toward those things that are true, noble, right, pure, lovely, admirable, excellent, and praiseworthy. For example, an older adult worried about developing Alzheimer's disease might write, "What is true is that God has promised to never leave or forsake me" or "What is lovely is that God has given me a wonderful family." This activity not only gives adults an opportunity to share their worries with a few trusted friends but also, even more important, empowers them to focus their thoughts on God.

**Self-Reliance** Most adults have become quite competent at taking care of themselves and their problems. Car doesn't start? Take it to a repair shop. Have a headache? Take some medicine. Nothing cooked for dinner? Go to a restaurant. And then there are more serious things: Marriage struggling? Go to counseling. Children disobeying? Revoke their privileges.

The problem with all these answers is that we feel like we don't really need God in our lives. There are lots of things we can take care of on our own. And yet God's desire is that we be completely dependent on Him. He wants us to need Him and Him alone.

The losses and challenges associated with aging can persuade older adults to throw themselves on God. Even though people fight it, aging cannot be reversed. Physical health does decline, aging parents need care, and loved ones do die. In these circumstances, when people have nowhere else to turn, we can point them to a deeper dependence on God, and in turn they will find peace and intimacy with Him. "My soul finds rest in God alone; my salvation comes from Him. He alone is my rock and my salvation; He is my fortress, I will never be shaken" (Psalm 62:1–2).

## Helping Older Adults Mature in Their Faith

We may want to take the easy way out and embrace the belief that it will be too hard for older adults to change in any of the above-mentioned areas. We may be guilty of saying, "That's just the way older people are." But as spiritual shepherds, we must develop a passion for loving, challenging, admonishing, and encouraging people to grow in their faith.

First, acknowledge that the changes and difficulties experienced by people in later life can reveal areas that need growth. This is a good thing! The Bible points out that trials actually help people mature in their faith. It is our privilege to walk with adults who are in this season of life and help them use this time to grow deeper in their relationship with the Lord.

Second, be patient with people. We are looking for evidence of change, not perfection. God meets us where we are and encourages us to go further. Everyone is in a different place spiritually. We are partnering with the Holy Spirit in this work, but it is God who brings about change.

As we pray for the Holy Spirit to work in the lives of boomers, we can encourage them to be seeking God on a regular basis. Some questions to ask include "Are they praying? Reading and meditating on Scripture? Journaling? Serving?" Practicing these spiritual disciplines (and others) helps position people for growth.

One small group leader encouraged group members to read the Bible during the week and write down what God was teaching them. Then he asked the participants in the weekly group meeting to tell how God was working in their lives. Most of the group members embraced this, but a married couple in their early sixties resisted. They said they didn't want to do this and were mostly interested in fellowship at the group meetings. This is a fairly obvious sign that this couple are not maturing in their walk with God. It's also a poignant reminder that even though this man and woman were older, they were not the most spiritually mature members of the group.

Sometimes it is appropriate to admonish someone during a one-on-one conversation. I distinctly remember a woman in her early seventies who was involved in the ministry I led at a megachurch. She attended multiple Bible studies and came to church regularly, yet she was critical of nearly everything and everyone and was sometimes downright mean. After an incident in which she spoke in an unkind and demeaning manner to my administrative assistant, I met with her and challenged her attitude and Christian example. Doing this sort of thing is difficult for most of us, but it may be the best way to shepherd someone. A person who professes to be a believer must be held to a higher standard.

We also need to ensure that our preaching and teaching addresses the spiritual topics and life issues affecting boomers. For example, when preaching on selfishness, we should give examples of how selfishness manifests itself in the lives of young adults *and* older adults. Too often the illustrations we share relate to only one particular age group.

Another way to help boomers grow is by persuading them to take action regarding what they learn in a sermon or lesson. We teach in order that people will learn, and as they learn, we should expect to see change.

Our daughter is in kindergarten, and she is learning basic reading skills. The teacher (and her parents) do not just talk about reading; we actually expect her to be able to do it! We are seeing the result of our teaching as she begins to recognize words and write the letters of the alphabet.

As adults, we get lazy. People take in information, but it does not result in any changes in attitudes, behaviors, or thoughts.

One way to help aging adults do something with what they've learned is to have them verbalize how the topic relates to something personal in their lives. Reggie McNeal calls this "debriefing." He gives this example in his book *Missional Renaissance*: "After we preach a sermon, we should ask people to declare to one or two people seated around them what they will take away from the message. Or perhaps we ask them to state one or two things they will do with what they've just heard or one or two things they will do differently based on the truth that has just been shared with them."[7]

Another way to help adults put into action what they've learned is to provide opportunities for them to practice. If the teaching was on being a good steward of your time and treasures, provide older adults with the opportunity to give a portion of their retirement income to a mission project and offer a short-term mission trip for them to participate in.

Finally, look at every activity, event, service project, and conversation as a divine opportunity for older adults to go deeper in their faith. Whether it be a special dinner at church, a hiking trip, or a day of raking leaves for the elderly, each of these activities can be used to draw people to God.

A small church in the Midwest has a monthly lunch gathering for older women in the church. This informal time affords these widowed women the chance to connect with others and enjoy a meal. For many of them, it is the highlight of their month. At one month's gathering, the women began talking about the hurt they were experiencing over their pastor's dismissal. They had not been provided with any explanation and were feeling left out and confused. One woman read a verse she found inspiring in her own quiet time with the Lord: "He will be the sure foundation for your times, a rich store of salvation and wisdom and knowledge; the fear of the Lord is the key to this treasure" (Isaiah 33:6). Her willingness to share opened up a door for a spiritual conversation that encouraged and challenged these ladies. Something as simple as a planned lunch became a significant moment for these women to grow in trusting God through all circumstances.

## Finishing Well

Pastor John Piper was a young boy when he would hear his dad preach and tell about the old man who had been hard and resistant to the gospel for many years but finally opened his heart and accepted Christ. Piper says that even as this man talked with his father and gave his life to Christ, he still sobbed and cried saying, "I've wasted it. I've wasted it."[8]

Aging causes people to reflect on their lives. Have they accomplished what they wanted to? Are they leaving the legacy they want to leave? Do they have any regrets? As older adults answer these questions, they are prompted to make changes—changes such as spending more time with family, volunteering in the community, or giving money to a worthy cause. They hope that in doing these things, they can find purpose for their life today and rectify mistakes they made in the past.

Our privilege, as well as our responsibility, is to help older adults not waste the remaining years of their lives, whether this means praying and leading them to Christ for the very first time or helping them find their way back to God after years of being away from Him or exhorting them to grow in their faith or challenging them to give selflessly to God's purposes in this world.

Whatever we have to do, we must make the spiritual lives of the members of this generation a priority. We must do all we can to help them finish well.

# 9

# MELDING THE GENERATIONS

Not long ago, a friend invited me to her Monday night church-affiliated small group. Let me give you a snapshot of who was there:

Scott and Kristy: Leaders of the group. In their forties. Married twenty-five years. Both work in corporate America. Have two college-age daughters.

Beth: Single woman, age twenty-six. Manager of a women's retail clothing store.

Joe and Angie: In their forties. Married nineteen years. Work for a parachurch ministry and own an event-planning business. Have a three-year-old son.

Doug and Barb: Retired couple in their early seventies. Married thirty-eight years. Regularly watch their grandchildren while the parents work. Host the small group in their home.

Larry and Donna: Relative newcomers to the church, in their sixties. Married twenty-three years. Both working. This is the first small group they've joined.

Susan: Single woman, age twenty-six. Intensive care unit nurse.

Jerry and Debbie: Newlyweds in their thirties (married one year). Expecting their first child.

Catherine and Kevin: Newlyweds around age forty (married one year). Both in demanding careers. No kids.

Marla: Single woman, age sixty. Works for an assisted living company in the marketing department. Was invited by her coworker, Kevin, to participate in the group.

Did you pick up on the fact that this small group has members ranging in age from people in their twenties to those in their seventies? In talking with these adults, I discovered that a few of them had never noticed the intergenerational nature of their group until I pointed it out. One of the women said to me, "I feel like this group is ageless. In fact, I don't really see the ages."

As the members began to reflect on the various ages within the group, they started to realize that the positive benefits of their intergenerational group far outnumbered the drawbacks. Learning from the life experiences of others, hearing different perspectives on a topic, and feeling a part of a family were just a few of the plusses they mentioned.

This group is one of twenty-three small groups at a church with a weekend attendance of about one thousand people. Interestingly, of the twenty-three groups, only two are intergenerational. In talking with church leaders around the country, I've discovered that this is not uncommon. Small groups are often arranged by age, and so are most classes in churches that use Sunday school as a method for connecting people. Churches may have a few token intergenerational classes or groups, but the majority are age-segregated.

Despite the lack of intergenerational ministries, most people agree that intergenerational relationships are important and valuable. But why discuss this topic in a book primarily focused on one particular generation?

Just as effective ministry with older adults will focus on service and spiritual growth, ministry with aging baby boomers must also include an intergenerational component. Boomers want and need to be challenged to use the later years of their lives to make a significant difference. Most older adults have talents and experiences to share, but without intergenerational connections, their impact is limited.

## Overcoming Age Barriers

A number of age barriers in our society and in our churches keep the generations apart. For one thing, *we live in an age-segregated society*. The educational system is set up so that children spend large amounts of time in school interacting with other children. Young adults are often working with other young adults, and older adults interact with others who are older. Communities set up programs and services based on age, such as a senior center for the older residents of the neighborhood and a youth facility for those who are younger. The assumption has been that it is easier to meet the specific needs of people if they are grouped by age.

It is also more common today for families to live apart from one another, separated by many miles, which means that even in families, generations may not have as much contact as they used to. People move because of job opportunities, a desire to live in a bigger or smaller city, or to pursue a different way of life. My husband has a brother in Missouri, a sister in Alaska, and a brother in Washington, while we and his mother both live in Nebraska (though in two different cities). In the past, adults were not as likely to move away from their families of origin, and so it was typical for the generations to interact on a daily basis.

Many churches also use age as a method for grouping people. In part, the baby boom generation influenced this trend because leaders saw the unique needs of this large group of young people and responded with age-specific ministries. As noted earlier, Sunday school and small group ministries are often based on age. You may find a class for the "twenty-somethings," one for the "young marrieds," and another for "retirees." The belief has been that people of the same age have similar needs and are dealing with the same life issues and therefore can best be served if grouped together. At times this kind of segmentation can be beneficial. There is value to spending time with others who are in a similar season of life. I benefit from having a few friends who are also moms of young children, but I equally value the close relationship I have with a fifty-something woman who has grand-children. We need both.

Sometimes an entire church strategy will target a specific age group, which leads to an absence of intergenerational relation-ships. Just as the marketing world will instruct you to narrow your audience so as better to reach potential consumers of a certain product, many churches believe they have to create a church that responds to the needs and desires of one specific generation. Another church strategy that can lead to genera-tional separation is the use of multiple services, each with a different worship style that caters to the particular musical tastes and preferences of adults. As members of each generation gravi-tate toward the service that resonates with them, the opportunity for intergenerational connections diminishes.

*Exchange theory* may be a second reason why intergenera-tional ministry is missing in many churches. This theory states that individuals and groups seek to maximize rewards and mini-mize costs.[1] People will maintain an interaction or a relationship if it continues to be more rewarding than costly. When geron-tology emerged as an academic discipline, exchange theory became one way of explaining why older people withdrew from relationships with younger people, why older adults were avoided, and why old age was seen as something negative. The belief was that older adults do not give as much as they receive, and therefore the exchange is not even.

For example, research has shown that few medical students choose geriatrics as their area of focus. Working with older adults doesn't sound as glamorous as being a pediatric neurosurgeon, nor does it pay as well. Many church pastors do not include older adult ministry in their budget or hire a staff member for this area. In both of these cases, the perception is that what will be given is greater than what will be received. To put it bluntly, many of us act as if old age is a liability rather than an asset. Is it possible that we think we receive more from someone young than from someone old? Is there more excitement over a young family joining the church as opposed to a seventy-five-year-old widow?

After speaking at an older adult retreat on the subject of sharing our lives with every generation, I was approached by a seventy-eight-year-old man named Jim, who told me about his weekly 6:30 A.M. breakfast with three other men who are in their thirties and forties. The men had been meeting to discuss aspects of the Christian life when they approached Jim and asked him to join their group. He said to me, "I told them I didn't have much to offer, but they said they wanted to ask me questions and get my input on things."

I remember thinking to myself, "Well, of course they want to spend time with you! You are a vibrant, articulate, encouraging Christian man with a lot of wisdom. And you are just plain fun to be around!" Exchange theory implies that these young men, who are doctors and professionals in the community, will not receive as much from Jim as they will give to him. What do you think?

A final barrier to intergenerational ministry is simply *a lack of understanding and appreciation for each generation*. You've probably heard people make comments like "What is going on with these young people today!" or "I don't have anything in common with those older folks!" Some refer to this disconnect between the generations as a "generation gap"—meaning that two or more generations have very different views on such things as fashion, politics, music, and morality. Take, for instance, the 2008 presidential election, in which the younger generation was far more likely than the older generation to vote for Barack Obama.[2] This same type of generational difference was felt in the 1960s among young baby boomers and their parents over such issues as women's rights and the Vietnam War.

There is no question that the generation we are a part of shapes us. The way we approach our jobs, our time with family, our finances, and our leisure pursuits are all influenced by the period of history in which we live. For example, many of those in the builder generation lived through the Great Depression. Because of this, they tend to be savers who are very frugal regardless of how much money they have tucked away. It seems absurd today that my grandmother cleaned out Vienna sausage cans and had us use them as drinking glasses. But she was poor for much of her life and learned to use everything available in order to survive. Younger generations cannot appreciate this unless they learn about the life circumstances of older generations.

The reverse is also true. Members of the older generation will be better able to accept those who are younger after learning about the circumstances affecting the young people's lives. Younger generations today have been so greatly influenced by technology that if they fail to keep up with the latest technological fads, they may find themselves without a social network of friends. This realization may help older adults be more sympathetic when seeing young people sending text messages or chatting on cell phones.

All of us are marked by the things we've experienced and the time period in which we were born. This affects how we view the world and how we view church. Generations that understand one another will be better able to love one another and ultimately work together in fulfilling God's mission on earth.

There is no way around the fact that barriers exist in our culture that keep the generations from connecting. More than any institution besides the family, the church has the framework in place to be highly intergenerational. But achieving this goal won't be easy. Working toward a more intergenerational approach to ministry will require effort and determination. So the question begs to be asked: Is it worth it?

## What Are the Benefits?

In the absence of relationships, most of us rely on stereotypes to tell us how to think and feel about certain groups of people. We may categorize a person in all kinds of ways—according to education, age, social class, race, or gender, for example—and depending on our past experiences with people in these categories, we form an initial impression, be it positive, negative, or neutral. But as we get to know the person as a unique individual, our perception will likely change.

This was clearly illustrated to me as I read the book *Same Kind of Different as Me*, about the close friendship formed between a wealthy art dealer and a homeless black man.[3] When they first met, neither man was interested in forming any type of relationship. But through a series of circumstances and the prayers of the art dealer's wife, they began to forge a friendship. As the men spent time talking over coffee, sharing their life stories, praying for each other, and serving together, the bond between them grew. Over time, they focused less on their differences and more on what they had in common, and eventually they established a lifelong friendship based on unconditional love.

There is no question that mixing the generations is *one of the best ways to break age-related stereotypes*. In Chapter Two, I mentioned that my gerontology students are required to interview two different older adults during the semester in order to gain a better understanding of the lives of older people. Often they will report that they originally thought the assignment would be boring and the interviewees would be "stuck in their ways," hard of hearing, and grumpy. Most students are surprised by how much they enjoy the experience and the discovery that older adults are actually a lot of fun! Some students even make plans to see the individuals again after the classroom requirement has been met.

Older adults may also hold negative stereotypes about young people. They can assume that all "kids" are reckless or lazy, but upon talking with the young people, they discover something completely different. It's good for older adults to realize the pressures young people face today, such as parents' divorce or financial worries. On the other hand, it's healthy for my students to hear about their grandparents (or other older adults) who eloped or broke their curfew or wrecked their dad's car.

When people really get to know one another, there is no longer a need to rely on stereotypes. Instead, true friendships develop, and young and old accept each other as individuals.

Building intergenerational relationships is also *a logical way for faith to be shared*. Throughout the Bible, God instructed His people to pass on to the next generation all they had seen or heard or experienced. Over and over in Scripture, we see examples of this happening. In the book of Joshua, we read that God stopped the flow of the waters so that the Israelites could cross the Jordan River and enter the Promised Land. After this miracle, Joshua instructs each of the twelve tribes to take a stone and build a memorial, so that

> in the future, when your descendants ask their fathers, "what do these stones mean?" tell them, "Israel crossed the Jordan on dry ground." For the Lord your God dried up the Jordan before you until you crossed over. The Lord your God did to the Jordan just what He had done to the Red Sea. . . . He did this so that all the people of the earth might know that the hand of the Lord is powerful and so that you might always fear the Lord your God [Joshua 4:21–24].

Deuteronomy 32 records the words of Moses that he sang to the whole assembly of Israel before he passed the mantle of leadership to Joshua. In verse 7 he says, "Remember the days of old; consider the generations long past. Ask your father and he will tell you, your elders and they will explain to you." Moses commanded the people to learn from the previous generations, even asking this older generation to explain the works of God.

King David indicated that being able to tell the next generation about God was one of his greatest desires. He said in Psalm 71:18, "Even when I am old and gray, do not forsake me, O God, till I declare your power to the next generation, your might to all who are to come."

In the normal occurrences of daily life, it was assumed that young and old would be interacting. And during time spent together, discussions about faith would naturally occur.

About a year after our daughter, Ella, was born, my husband and I went away to a Christian retreat center for some rest and healing. I had suffered with postpartum depression, and things were tough. I spent a lot of my time walking alongside a creek, praying and crying out to God. The outdoors and God's presence with me brought restoration to my soul. To remind me of this special time, I gathered some rocks from the creek, and upon returning home, I put them in a decorative jar by the kitchen sink. One day, when Ella was about four years old, she said, "Mommy, why do you have rocks by the sink?" I responded, "Oh, they remind me of a special trip with your daddy." Later, when she asked me the same question again, I seized the opportunity to elaborate: "Mommy was going through a hard time, and God helped her. Those rocks remind me that God is always my helper. And He is your helper, too."

Intergenerational ministry is not just about the young and old hanging out together. In the Bible, generations connected to pass on the things of God. Young people need to hear about God's faithfulness so they can grow stronger in their own faith, and this happens best when multiple generations are regularly interacting.

Another benefit of establishing intergenerational connections is that *the church becomes more unified*. I've heard some church leaders refer to the age separation in our churches as a "silo" approach to ministry, with different age groups of people separated from one another, each doing their own thing. But Galatians 6:10 serves as a reminder that the church is a family and we are to interact regularly, learning from one another, not siloed into certain categories. Silos can create disunity.

The relationship between youth ministry and the church at large has been a common silo approach to ministry. The Fuller Youth Institute recently reported that many young people who once were highly involved in a church youth group during junior high and high school stopped participating in church as young adults.[4] Many of these teenagers were in separate worship services with their own music, fellowship, and teaching and rarely engaged with the larger church. Relationships with anyone outside their age group became almost nonexistent.

This format for youth ministry can cause disunity within the church and even drive young adults away from the church because they don't know how to connect with the larger church body. Although age-specific programming can be useful, there are also times when all age groups need to be together. In fact, Fuller found a strong link between young people's staying in church after graduating from high school and their involvement in intergenerational relationships and worship.

Cedar Mills Bible Church in Portland, Oregon, is intentionally working to create an intergenerational environment by having a monthly worship service called Generations Unite. Nearly all of the 150 high school students are present in the service, many of them as part of the worship band. Junior high students serve communion and serve as ushers alongside sixty-year-old adults. All of the different age groups participate fully in the worship experience.

A unified church, where all generations regularly interact, also helps people live out 1 Corinthians 12:12. This verse reminds us that the church is made up of many parts, but we form one body in Christ. We need one another, and we need what each age group has to offer.

Council Road Baptist Church in Bethany, Oklahoma, has a Sunday morning class with adults of all ages and backgrounds, including newlyweds, grandparents, and single adults. Everyone in the class is able to learn from and support everyone else. The couples in the class with young children can look to those who are older for advice. One single mom in the group has found people from the class who are willing to help with child care, plumbing problems, and even financial needs. All of the class members enjoy getting together in each other's homes, serving with one another at church on Wednesday nights, and helping each other during times of crisis.

## Making It a Reality

Effective intergenerational ministry begins with recognizing the benefits and then intentionally deciding to become a church that embraces all ages. Often an intergenerational focus expands from one ministry, such as the youth ministry or the older adult ministry. For example, an older adult Sunday school class decides to send care packages to the church's young people during finals week, or the high school youth group organizes a Valentine's Day banquet for the older adults. These are great activities—but it takes more than one activity to become a multigenerational church. Truly becoming an intergenerational church means that the leadership must adopt this philosophy in all aspects of the church. Once we've made this commitment, specific strategies can help us break down age barriers and make intergenerational connections a reality.

A great way to connect the generations is *encouraging them to serve together on a worthy cause*. Working shoulder to shoulder on a common project helps people see past their differences and focus on something greater than themselves. Short-term mission trips, work with the local homeless shelter, or a project with Habitat for Humanity can all have teams that include people of all ages.

Even something as basic as leading a Sunday school class provides an opportunity for intergenerational serving to occur. I was reminded of this when I talked with Mark, the father of a fifteen-year-old young man named Caleb. I learned that on Sunday mornings, Caleb gets to church at First Baptist in West Monroe, Louisiana, by 7:15. While many teenagers might grumble about getting up so early, Caleb looks forward to the ministry that awaits him. Week after week, he sacrifices his sleep to teach the 8:00 A.M. Sunday school class for three-year-olds alongside an eighty-one-year-old man affectionately known as Mr. Charlie.

Mr. Charlie has been teaching this class for more than fifteen years, and twelve years ago he actually had Caleb as one of his three-year-old students. Now as a helper to Mr. Charlie, Caleb and this older man enjoy a relationship that goes beyond the one hour they serve together on Sunday. Charlie calls Caleb regularly and celebrates his school achievements. The two of them exchange Christmas presents and enjoy a rich friendship.

Chapelwood United Methodist Church in Houston, Texas, also recognizes the value of multiple generations serving together, especially on the mission field. For more than six years, women of all ages have spent one week in Tapachula, Mexico, ministering with the children of prisoners as well as some of the mothers of these children. One year, there were eight women on the trip, five of them over the age of fifty. Each of the women made a unique contribution. Some of the younger women spoke Spanish fluently, which helped in communicating with those they were serving. A few of the older women used their sewing skills, while one woman set up a blog so that the Chapelwood congregation could follow the trip online. Others on the team nurtured the children one-on-one while some planned group activities for the children. The age diversity of the team enhanced the ministry by giving different perspectives and approaches in working with the children and their mothers.

Almost any service project can use the help of people of all ages. A ninety-year-old and a ten-year-old can work together to fill backpacks with school supplies for children in need, and a sixty-year-old and a twenty-year-old can travel together to visit residents in a nursing home. The work they are doing for others creates a bond between the generations. And in serving together, they are able to learn from each other and grow in their relationship with Christ.

A second way of connecting the generations is *forming groups according to similar interests rather than age*. One principle you may recall from earlier in this book is that leading-edge boomers do not want their age to dictate what class or group they can join. This actually seems to be the case for all generations—no one likes to be labeled or categorized.

A discovery I made after talking with the small group members I mentioned at the beginning of this chapter is that many of the members intentionally chose to be in a diverse group. Some of them didn't want to be a part of the church's singles ministry, and others told me that they often feel intimidated talking about difficult life issues with their peers. Susan, one of the single twenty-somethings in the group said, "I was recently going through the challenging process of buying my first house. It was much easier to talk with people older than me because there was no jealousy or judgment on their part. They didn't compare their lives with mine, as some of my peers were doing. My older friends in the group simply listened and offered advice from their own life experience."

Most of us enjoy having opportunities to participate in activities and talk about issues that transcend our age and season of life. I am a part of a book club at our church in which women of a wide range of ages participate. Our common interest in reading good books and coming together to discuss them is what brought us together; our stage in life is not a factor. Other churches organize groups around motorcycle riding, photography, and scrapbooking to reach out to people who are interested in those particular hobbies. As people come together over common interests, meaningful relationships can develop that cross generational lines.

Another way of melding the generations is *encouraging older adults to intentionally pray for young people and vice versa.* A few months ago, I talked with an older woman named Peggy who had been praying for a young woman for a number of years. The relationship began when Peggy and her husband attended a luncheon for adults over fifty at their church at which they were encouraged to choose a picture of a teenager displayed on the wall and begin praying for this young person. Peggy selected the photograph of a young girl named Sara who was a member of the church. Soon after this, Peggy phoned Sara and told her she would be praying for her. Peggy told me, "We bonded instantly. She was so happy to have me in her life, and in turn she made me feel like I was truly making a difference." At the time, Sara's mother was undergoing chemotherapy treatments, and Peggy became a support to Sara. As the years passed, Sara moved out of state to attend college, but Peggy continued praying. Peggy even flew across the country to attend Sara's wedding.

When we consistently and sincerely pray for someone, our capacity to care about that individual grows. Generational differences that used to cause arguments (such as loud music or body piercing) become immaterial as we begin to love one another as Christ loved. Prayer helps mold our hearts to be more like Christ and in turn to have His compassion and mercy for people who are difficult to love.

As church leaders, we can help people establish these prayer connections. It may be as simple as gathering names from the youth or children's ministry and matching these young people with an older adult. Planning a special event with the purpose of introducing the prayer partners to one another would give young and old a chance to share their individual prayer needs. Over time, adults and youth should be encouraged to tell the stories of how a prayer was answered or how the prayer partnership has blessed their lives. Doing this in a Bible study setting or some other small gathering will help hold people accountable to continue in prayer.

We do not always have to formally match people in prayer partnerships. We can also use worship services, classes, and Bible studies to suggest that members choose individuals from their own lives to pray for, such as a young person in the neighborhood, a grandchild, or a young family from the church.

Obviously, people can pray for the physical needs of others, including their health and safety, but we cannot neglect showing people how to pray for spiritual needs. One way of doing this is teaching people to pray Scripture for someone else. For example, when I pray for our daughter, I often pray the words of Mark 12:30: "God, help Ella grow up to love you with all of her heart and soul and mind and strength." If you know people who are worrying about a difficult decision, pray that they will "trust the Lord with all their heart and lean not on their own understanding" (Proverbs 3:5–6). The words of the Bible are powerful in defeating the schemes of the enemy, and praying Scripture also ensures that we are praying God's will over someone's life.

We can help people pray God's Word by encouraging them to notice what verses are mentioned in sermons and lessons that apply to the people they are praying for. We can also teach people to use a concordance to find out what God has to say about a certain subject and then show them how to frame the selected verses into prayers. People can be challenged to take this a step further and send an encouraging note to the person they are praying for, including the specific verse.

*Hosting strategic intergenerational events* can also be an effective way of fostering intergenerational relationships. These are planned events to which two or more generations are invited in order to interact and enjoy one another. The most successful intergenerational activities tend to have three things in common. First of all, these events should be fun for all participants regardless of age. Whether it is a bowling tournament, a tea party, or a magic show, each generation needs to find the activity pleasurable.

Second, the organizers of the event should provide some ready-made questions that permit the age groups to engage easily in conversation. For example, if the event includes a dinner, place a list of these questions at the table for young and old to discuss while eating. If the event involves something like listening to a comedian or viewing a movie, allow time for people to break into small groups and discuss the questions. Typical questions might be "What was a favorite present you received as a child?" "Where did you go on vacation when you were young?" and "When was the first time God became real to you?"

Third, the event should encourage relationships to continue after the event is over. Cedar Mills Bible Church hosts an annual miniature golf outing in which golf teams are made up of one older adult and two high school students. Each team is photographed, and everyone receives a copy of the picture with the names and phone numbers of the teammates. The prizes that are awarded include gift cards to coffee shops or ice-cream stores in order to encourage the older adult and the teens to reconnect at a later time. According to Dave McElheran, older adult ministries pastor at the church, 75 percent of the golf teams maintain at least an acquaintance relationship, and about 25 percent develop a lasting relationship that continues and goes deeper.

Another important component of intergenerational ministry is *asking adults to tell their stories*. Telling faith stories is one of the best ways to pass on the things of God. Deuteronomy 11:18–20 clearly states that when the generations are together, those who are older should be teaching those who are younger about God.

Grace Presbyterian Church in Houston, Texas, recognized the power of preserving the individual stories of people and took on a book project called *Stories of Grace*. The pages in this book tell the individual stories of twenty-four people—children, young adults, middle-aged adults, and older adults. Each person was interviewed and asked to specifically consider the question "Where are the handprints of God in my life?" The interviews were then edited and written in the form of stories. Doug Ferguson, the senior pastor of Grace Presbyterian, wrote in the foreword of the book, "Among the things that hold families together are the stories that are told and passed on from generation to generation. . . . They are the stories of God's mighty acts among us, stories of faithfulness and stories of grace."[5]

Some churches use video to capture the stories of people and then show these recordings at appropriate times to the entire congregation. In other instances, live testimonies during a Sunday service may provide the best opportunity for people to pass on a piece of their faith.

But it's often not as easy as simply asking people to share their stories. Adults may need to be prompted to bring to mind the moments in their lives when they recognized God at work. This may work best if older adults are asked to write their memories down.

Writing Your Memories classes are becoming increasingly popular. Senior centers, colleges, and other community groups frequently offer these courses; churches do as well. An Internet search or a quick look in a Christian bookstore will reveal a number of resources that are useful for helping people write their memories. Some churches even create their own legacy workbooks or booklets, as I mentioned in Chapter Four, that include questions to aid in the writing process.

Recalling memories will also mean bringing to mind difficult circumstances, but these stories are important because they can help a young person grow in faith. Young people need to hear stories about how God was faithful during times of financial difficulty or when experiencing infertility or when coping with a loss. This empowers members of the younger generation to more fully trust God and His provision in the current circumstances of their own lives.

Intergenerational small groups and Sunday school classes can provide a natural place for these connections to occur. Even a planned event can open up these kinds of significant conversations.

First Evangelical Free Church in Fullerton, California, hosts an event called Back to the Future when a few older adults attend a regular youth group activity. The entire group is broken into small groups so that one or two older adults can interact with a small number of students. Often the older adults will bring their yearbooks, letter jackets, and report cards for the young people to see. The students ask questions and simply talk with the older adults about dating, family issues, and matters of faith.

*Integrating all ages in the worship service* is an additional way of becoming more intergenerational. The church should be a place where everyone is loved, accepted, and regarded as having equal value and importance. Though nearly all of us would agree with that statement, it nevertheless takes effort to make it happen on an ongoing basis. Would an outsider observe that your church truly is a church for all ages? A concrete way of communicating this is by having people of different ages participate in the worship service. Even if you have different services for different musical preferences, you can still involve people of a variety of ages. Some churches have a full orchestra at the traditional service, with high school students and older adults playing the instruments. There are seventy-year-old adults who sing in the contemporary choir or play the guitar in the worship band alongside musicians in their twenties. Young people and older adults can share the responsibility of serving communion or being an usher. The key is to visually demonstrate that every age group is necessary and important.

A final way to bridge the generations and help meaningful relationships form is by *educating people as to the uniqueness of each generation*. A sermon or series of sermons that focus on the characteristics of each generation will help church members appreciate generational differences and learn to relate to one another more fully. Education can also occur in small groups and classes where each generation is discussed and people can reflect on how they've seen generational differences manifested in their own lives.

## Generational Wars or Generational Peace?

There are a number of people inside and outside the political world who devote their time and energy to something called the generational equity debate. Proponents of generational equity believe that older adults have received an unfair amount of public resources, making them more financially stable than younger generations. Some would even go so far as to say that we spend too much on the older generation and not enough on children. Programs such as Social Security and Medicare can certainly cause us to wonder if this might be true. In some communities, when a school bond issue is voted down, people feel that the result came from the elderly voters who only care about their own needs and not those of future generations. Some leaders fear that with the boomer population entering the later years of life, we will witness generational wars over finances and programs.

We might not like to admit it, but many churches experience generational wars too. Who should receive the biggest chunk of budget dollars for ministry? What musical style should we use in our services? Who should our target audience be? Who will get the best room or best time slot for their event? It goes on and on.

As multiple generations work, worship, serve, and play together, the result will be that people lay down their own self-centeredness and take up the attitude of Christ. True, we may have to do church a little differently, but when all ages are regularly interacting and loving one another, God is honored, and we become an example to our hurting world.

# CONCLUSION:
# AN UNCHARTED OPPORTUNITY

Not long ago, I met a retired man who was a living example of the vision we hope all adults will embrace. He was serving in various ministries in his local church and had a passion for life that was contagious. When I asked him why he served in such a significant way during his retirement years, he told me a story.

"When my granddaughter was a little girl, I used to sing a song to her that went like this:

> One, two, three, four, five, six, seven,
> All good girls go to heaven.
> When they get there, they will say,
> "We love Jesus every day."

"One day, I overheard her singing the song in another room. She sang:

> One, two, three, four, five, six, seven,
> All good grandpas go to heaven.
> When they get there, they will say,
> "GOLF, GOLF, GOLF, GOLF, every day!"

At this point, I cracked up laughing, but he looked me straight in the eyes with a serious look on his face and said, "Amy, in that moment, I saw myself through the eyes of my granddaughter. She saw what my passion was, and this was not the legacy I wanted to leave."

He proceeded to tell me about the changes he made in his life after this realization. He chose to spend less time golfing and instead looked for activities he could participate in with his family. For example, he made it his routine to pick up his grandsons from school a few days a week so that they could play tennis together, a sport his grandsons enjoyed. The time he spent with them gave him the opportunity to have meaningful conversations regarding what they were experiencing at school and with their friends. He looked for ways to spend time with his granddaughter and the other members of his family, taking a genuine interest in their lives and demonstrating the love of Christ.

His new focus also led him to be more active in church, participating in Bible studies and classes and in the process growing closer to God. He began serving people in the community, sharing his life with those in need.

His story typifies the dream I have for every single person over the age of fifty. It is a dream where older adults are motivated to give their lives away to people needing God's grace. A dream where aging is not feared but rather welcomed as a God-ordained season of life.

It is a dream where adults are telling their life stories to the next generation—proclaiming God's faithfulness and provision. A dream where older adults find purpose and meaning through a relationship with Jesus Christ. A dream where no one is marginalized because of age.

It is a dream where older adults continue to grow in intimacy with God. A dream where older adults are fully using all of their talents, gifts, and abilities to make a major Kingdom impact.

God began to stir this dream in me at a young age, and by the time I graduated from high school and entered Bible college, this spark to make a difference in the world of older adult ministry was being fanned into a flame. Even as a college student, I wrote papers, read books, and pursued internships in this emerging area. People thought I was crazy and couldn't believe that a competent nineteen-year-old woman with a year of college under her belt would want to jump into the almost unheard-of arena of ministry with people over fifty. Shouldn't I be using my ministry gifts serving youth? Or maybe I should look into women's ministry or children's ministry?

But God had a grip on me, and I had a burning passion to see the entire landscape of aging and older adult ministry change. Over the years, I have served as an older adult minister, pursued further education, taught classes, written articles, and done just about everything I could to speak this message. When I would become frustrated that no one was listening, voices would say, "The time isn't right," "The church isn't ready yet," "We'll get there one day."

Well, the day has finally come. The bulging numbers of adults marching into their fifth, sixth, and seventh decades of life is larger than it has ever been. Now is the time to make the dream come alive. Now is the time to unleash older adults to live out their God-given purpose. Now is the time to create effective ministries that reach out to adults over fifty. Now is the time to explore the possibilities.

Now is the time.

# NOTES

## Chapter One: A Wake-Up Call for the Church

1  Mark Senter, *The Coming Revolution in Youth Ministry: And Its Radical Impact on the Church* (Wheaton, Ill.: Victor Books, 1992), p. 142.

2  U.S. Department of Health and Human Services, Administration on Aging, "A Profile of Older Americans, 2008," http://www.mowaa.org/Document.Doc?id=69, p. 2.

3  Ibid.

4  Ibid., p. 3.

5  U.S. Census Bureau, "Selected Characteristics of Baby Boomers 42 to 60 Years Old in 2006," http://www.census.gov/population/www/socdemo/age/2006%20Baby%20Boomers.pdf, p. 20 (computed by averaging 78 million baby boomers turning sixty for eighteen years).

6  Bae Ji-Sook, "Seoul Is Aging Fast," *Korea Times*, Aug. 4, 2009, http://www.koreatimes.co.kr/www/news/nation/2009/08/113_49616.html

7  See David Hackett Fisher, *Growing Old in America* (Oxford: Oxford University Press, 1977). Some scholars suggest that Fisher's portrayal of aging in colonial America is not entirely accurate.

8  Harriet Brott, "In Search of Youth, Women Turning to Hormones," *Self*, Aug. 3, 2009, http://www.msnbc.msn.com/id/32034820/ns/health-skin_and_beauty

## Chapter Two: Not What You Thought

1 Federal Interagency Forum on Aging-Related Statistics, *Older Americans Update 2006: Key Indicators of Well-Being* (Washington, D.C.: U.S. Government Printing Office, May 2006), http://www.aoa.gov/agingstatsdotnet/Main_Site/Data/2006_Documents/OA_2006.pdf, p. 52.

2 Cary S. Kart, *The Realities of Aging: An Introduction to Gerontology*, 4th ed. (New York: Simon & Schuster, 1994), p. 9.

3 Stephen J. Cutler and Nicholas L. Danigelis, "Changes in Attitudes," in *Encyclopedia of Ageism*, ed. Erdman B. Palmore, Laurence Branch, and Diana K. Harris (Binghamton, N.Y.: Haworth Pastoral Press, 2005), pp. 63–66.

4 Gordon MacDonald, *Who Stole My Church? What to Do When the Church You Love Tries to Enter the 21st Century* (Nashville, Tenn.: Nelson, 2007), p. 53.

5 Sara E. Rix, "Employment," in *The Encyclopedia of Aging*, ed. George Maddox (New York: Springer, 2001), vol. 1, p. 333.

6 Gene D. Cohen, *The Creative Age: Awakening Human Potential in the Second Half of Life* (New York: Quill, 2001).

7 Barry Gurland, "Psychopathology," in *The Encyclopedia of Aging*, vol. 2, p. 845.

8 Jill Quadagno, *Aging and the Life Course*, 2nd ed. New York: McGraw-Hill, 2002), p. 188.

9 Barna Group, http://www.barna.org

10 Gary L. McIntosh, *One Church, Four Generations: Understanding and Reaching All Ages in Your Church* (Grand Rapids, Mich.: Baker Books, 2002), p. 45.

11 Barna Group, "Evangelism Is Most Effective Among Kids," Oct. 11, 2004, http://www.barna.org/barna-update/article/5-barna-update/196-evangelism-is-most-effective-among-kids

12 Kristen Gerencher, "Older Volunteers Seek Right Fit," *Wall Street Journal*, July 25, 2007.

13 Throughout this book, I will draw on numerous interviews that I conducted with churches across the country that are doing innovative older adult ministry. The bulk of this research was done in conjunction with Leadership Network in 2007 and 2008. For additional information on these churches, see the three concept papers of mine posted at http://www.leadnet.org/encoregeneration.

14 John W. Rowe and Robert L. Kahn, *Successful Aging* (New York: Dell, 1998), p. 3.

15 J. Kirk Gulledge, "Influences on Clergy Attitudes Toward the Aging," *Journal of Religious Gerontology*, 1991, 8(2), 63–77.

## Chapter Three: Aging Well

1 Rowe and Kahn, *Successful Aging*.

2 Gerontological Society of America, "Study Reveals Factors of Exceptional Health in Old Age" (press release), Oct. 27, 2008.

3 Nancy R. Hooyman and H. Asuman Kiyak, *Social Gerontology: A Multidisciplinary Perspective*, 8th ed. (Boston: Allyn & Bacon, 2008).

4 Maria E. Schmidt and others, "Physical Activity and Postmenopausal Breast Cancer: Effect Modification by Breast Cancer Subtypes and Effective Periods in Life," *Cancer Epidemiology, Biomarkers, and Prevention*, 2008, 17(12), 3402–3410.

5 Rowe and Kahn, *Successful Aging*, p. 109.

6 Ibid., p. 75.

7 Administration on Aging, "Good Nutrition! Essential for Health!!" May 2000, http://www.aoa.gov/naic/may2000/factsheets/nutrition.html

8 Alzheimer's Association, http://www.alz.org

9 New Tech Media, "Older Americans Fear Alzheimer's the Most, While Most Adults Fear Cancer," *Senior Journal.com*, May 31, 2006, http://seniorjournal.com/NEWS/Alzheimers/6-05-31-OlderAmericans.htm

## Chapter Four: Relationships and Responsibilities

1 J. Walker Smith and Ann Clurman, *Generation Ageless: How Baby Boomers Are Changing the Way We Live Today . . . and They're Just Getting Started* (New York: HarperCollins, 2007), p. 172.

2 Amy Goyer, "Grandparents Day 2008," *AARP.org,* Sept. 2008, http://www.aarp.org/family/articles/goyer_grandparents _day.html

3 Hooyman and Kiyak, *Social Gerontology,* p. 353.

4 Kathryn Zullo and Allan Zullo, *A Boomer's Guide to Grandparenting,* rev. ed. (Kansas City, Mo.: Andres McMeel, 2004), pp. 2–3.

5 Lydia Lum, "Handling 'Helicopter Parents,'" *Diverse Issues in Higher Education,* 2006, *23*(20), 40–43.

6 Administration on Aging, *A Profile of Older Americans, 2008* (Washington, D.C.: U.S. Department of Health and Human Services, 2008), http://www.aoa.gov/AoARoot/ Aging_Statistics/Profile/index.aspx

7 Carole Fleck, "Double Bind: As Boomers Juggle Work and Caring for Aging Parents, Business Pays Price," *AARP Bulletin,* May 2006, http://bulletin.aarp.org/yourhealth/care-giving/articles/cost_elder_care.html

8 For a more complete description of this program, see Amy Hanson, "Breaking Down the Age Barriers: How Some Churches Are Becoming Intentionally Inter-generational," July 24, 2008, http://www.leadnet.org/LC _EncoreGeneration.asp

9 Ken Dychtwald and Joe Flower, *Age Wave: How the Most Important Trend of Our Time Will Change Your Future* (New York: Bantam Books, 1990), pp. 212–214.

10 Connie Matthiessen, "Love and Marriage (and Caregiv-ing): Caring.com's Marriage Survey," *Caring.com,* n.d., http://www.caring.com/articles/love-and-marriage-when -caregiving

## Chapter Five: Retirement

1 David J. Ekerdt, "Born to Retire: The Foreshortened Life Course," *Gerontologist*, 2004, 44(1), 3–9.
2 Dora L. Costa, *The Evolution of Retirement: An American Economic History, 1880–1990* (Chicago: University of Chicago Press, 1998).
3 U.S. Bureau of Labor Statistics, *Employment Projections*, tab. 3.3: "Civilian Labor Force Participation Rates by Age, Sex, Race, and Ethnicity, 1988, 1998, 2008, and Projected 2018," 2008, http://www.bls.gov/emp/ep_table_303.pdf
4 Merrill Lynch, "'The New Retirement Survey' from Merrill Lynch Reveals How Baby Boomers Will Transform Retirement," press release, Feb. 22, 2005, http://www.ml.com/?id=7695_7696_8149_46028_46503_46635
5 Princeton Survey Research Associates International, "New Face of Work Survey: Executive Summary," June 2005, http://www.civicventures.org/publications/surveys/new_face_of_work/nfw_exec_summary.pdf
6 Cyclic and linear life cycles are discussed by Ken Dychtwald and Joe Flower in *Age Wave: How the Most Important Trend of Our Time Will Change Your Future.*
7 Robert N. Butler, *The Longevity Revolution: The Benefits and Challenges of Living a Long Life* (New York: Public Affairs, 2008), p. 241.
8 Fidelity Investments, "Fidelity Investments Estimates $240,000 Needed to Pay Health Care Costs in Retirement" (press release), Mar. 26, 2009, http://content.members.fidelity.com/Inside_Fidelity/fullStory/1,,7692,00.html
9 The consolidation approach was introduced by Robert Atchley; see his explanation in *Social Forces and Aging: An Introduction to Social Gerontology*, 8th ed. (Belmont, Calif.: Wadsworth, 1997), pp. 166–167.
10 New Tech Media, "Baby Boomers Worried About Money for Retirement," June 18, 2003, *Senior Journal.com*, http://

www.seniorjournal.com/NEWS/Features/3-06-18delweb
.htm

11 For more information about ministry in fifty-five-plus
living communities, see Amy Hanson, "Churches Responding
to the Age Wave: Top Innovations in Older Adult Ministry,"
Apr. 4, 2007, http://www.leadnet.org/LC_EncoreGeneration
.asp

12 Atchley, *Social Forces and Aging*, pp. 256–259.

13 James A. Thorson, *Aging in a Changing Society*, 2nd ed.
(Philadelphia: Brunner/Mazel, 2000), p. 318.

## Chapter Six: Letting Go of the "One Size Fits All" Mentality

1 Butler, *Longevity Revolution*, p. 245.

2 Emily Brandon, "When Does Old Age Begin?" *U.S. News &
World Report*, July 2, 2009, http://www.usnews.com/blogs/
planning-to-retire/2009/07/02/when-does-old-age-begin
.html

3 Frank Greve, "As Seniors Live Longer They Find 'Love
Expectancy' Also Grows," *McClatchy Newspapers*, June 16,
2008, http://www.mcclatchydc.com/homepage/story/44481
.html

## Chapter Seven: Serving

1 U.S. Bureau of Labor Statistics, "Volunteering in the United
States, 2009," Jan. 27, 2010, http://www.bls.gov/news
.release/volun.nr0.htm

2 "Boomers Show Entrepreneurial Spirit," *Business First of
Buffalo*, July 2, 2009, http://www.bizjournals.com/buffalo/
stories/2009/06/29/daily40.html

3 Mark A. Musick and John Wilson, *Volunteers: A Social Profile*
(Bloomington: Indiana University Press, 2008).

4 VolunteerMatch, *Great Expectations: Boomers and the Future
of Volunteering* (San Francisco: VolunteerMatch, 2008),

http://www.volunteermatch.org/nonprofits/resources/
greatexpectations/GreatExpectations_FullReport.pdf

5 Corporation for National and Community Service, "People All-Stars Among Us" (video), July 14, 2009, http://www .youtube.com/watch?v=dF79bghfm80

6 Bruce Bugbee, *What You Do Best in the Body of Christ: Discover Your Spiritual Gifts, Personal Style, and God-Given Passion*, rev. ed. (Grand Rapids, Mich.: Zondervan, 2005), p. 81.

7 Ken Dychtwald and Daniel J. Kadlec, *The Power Years: A User's Guide to the Rest of Your Life* (Hoboken, N.J.: Wiley, 2005).

8 Musick and Wilson, *Volunteers*.

## Chapter Eight: Matters of Faith

1 George Barna and Mark Hatch, *Boiling Point: Monitoring Cultural Shifts in the 21st Century* (Ventura, Calif.: Regal Books, 2001), p. 242.

2 Harold G. Koenig, *Aging and God: Spiritual Pathways to Mental Health in Midlife and Later Years* (Binghamton, N.Y.: Haworth Press, 1994), p. 428.

3 John S. Gomperts, "Serve America Act Will Help Boomers with Midlife Career Transitions," *Deseret News*, Apr. 21, 2009, http://www.deseretnews.com/article/705298602/Serve -America-Act-will-help-boomers.html

4 Kay Warren, *Dangerous Surrender: What Happens When You Say Yes to God* (Grand Rapids, Mich.: Zondervan, 2007), p. 203.

5 Ibid., p. 204.

6 Lloyd Reeb and Bill Wellons, *Unlimited Partnership: Igniting a Marketplace Leader's Journey to Significance* (Nashville, Tenn.: B&H, 2006), pp. 46–54.

7 Reggie McNeal, *Missional Renaissance: Changing the Scorecard for the Church* (San Francisco: Jossey-Bass, 2009), pp. 102–103.

8 John Piper, *Don't Waste Your Life* (Wheaton, Ill.: Crossway Books, 2007), pp. 11–12.

## Chapter Nine: Melding the Generations

1 James J. Dowd, "Aging as Exchange: A Preface to Theory," *Journal of Gerontology*, 1975, 30, 584–594.

2 "Study Finds Widening Generation Gap," *CBSNews.com*, June 29, 2009, http://www.cbsnews.com/stories/2009/06/29/national/main5122660.shtml

3 Ron Hall, Denver Moore, and Lynn Vincent, *Same Kind of Different as Me: A Modern-Day Slave, an International Art Dealer, and the Unlikely Woman Who Bound Them Together* (Nashville, Tenn.: Nelson, 2006).

4 "Is the Era of Age Segregation Over?" *Leadership Journal*, Summer 2009, pp. 43–47, http://www.christianitytoday.com/le/communitylife/discipleship/istheeraofagesegmentationover.html

5 For more information on sharing faith stories, see Amy Hanson, "Breaking Down the Age Barriers: How Some Churches Are Becoming Intentionally Intergenerational," July 24, 2008, at http://www.leadnet.orgLC_EncoreGeneration.asp

# ABOUT THE AUTHOR

Amy Hanson is a speaker, writer, and consultant with a passion to help older adults discover a life of Christ-centered meaning and purpose. She speaks throughout the United States to pastors, health care professionals, and older adults on the unique needs and opportunities of a graying America.

At the age of twenty-three, Amy became the full-time active adult minister at Central Christian Church in Las Vegas, Nevada, where for five years she led a ministry of over three hundred adults age fifty and older.

Amy has a bachelor's degree in Bible and family ministry from Manhattan Christian College, a master's degree in gerontology from Abilene Christian University, and a doctorate in human sciences from the University of Nebraska. She teaches several aging courses at the college level and has conducted research on volunteerism among older adults in the church.

Amy's experience also includes working with a Christian continuing-care retirement community as well as serving on the Speakers' Bureau for the Alzheimer's Association. She has written a number of articles on older adult ministry for Leadership Network, REV! and *Christian Standard*. She is currently a member of the CASA Network Writers' Panel and serves on the board of directors for Christian Homes, Inc.

Amy and her husband, Jon, live in Omaha, Nebraska, with their two children, Ella and Eli. You can learn more about Amy's ministry by visiting http://www.amyhanson.org.

# INDEX

# AMY HANSON
speaker • author • consultant

*"There is no one more qualified, more passionate, and more equipped to speak to the opportunities for unleashing an aging America to change the world."*
Gene Appel, Senior Pastor, Eastside Christian Church, Fullerton, CA

## Visit amyhanson.org

* Join on-going conversations about ministry with the new old
* Download a free discussion guide to use with *Baby Boomers and Beyond*
* Share stories of boomers making a significant Kingdom impact
* Invite Amy to speak at your church or consult with your leadership team

*"If you are serious about mobilizing the boomer generation for significant second half Kingdom work, I encourage you to get Amy on your team."*
Rev. Chris Holck, Encore Director of the
Evangelical Free Church of America

amyhanson.org